T0170549

ANGEL'S WING

ANGEL'S WING

A YEAR IN THE
SKIES OF VIETNAM

JOSEPH R. FINCH

Bartleby Press
Washington • Baltimore

ISBN 978-0-910155-45-8
Library of Congress Control Number: 2001135626

Printed in the United States of America

Published by:

Bartleby Press
8600 Foundry Street
Mill Box 2043
Savage, Maryland 20763
(800) 953-9929

To my Family: Monika, Nick and Tanya too

CONTENTS

ACKNOWLEDGMENTS

I want to thank my mother, Julia Finch, who waited patiently for my return. She saved every letter I wrote from Vietnam, maintained a scrapbook, and was a major force behind this book.

I also want to thank Chris Jensen for the photos that dress up *Angel's Wing*. All my photographs from Vietnam were destroyed in 1986.

Cover Photo

The cover photo is an extraction mission flown near "French Fort," about 10 kilometers north of Nui Ba Dinh. It was taken by a US Army Signal Corps photographer who had spent several days in the field under hostile fire with an infantry unit (4th of the 6th Infantry).

He snapped this photograph, came up to the aircraft and asked for a ride to Cu Chi. Hughey Weston, the aircraft commander, obliged so we put him on board. The photo appeared on Hughey's desk several days later along with a note saying "Thanks for the ride." No one saw the messenger or, as far as we know, ever saw the photographer again.

In the selection process for cover art for *Angel's Wing*, we chose this photograph, cropped from Hughey's original, which shows three aircraft on approach to the landing zone. I contacted the US Army Signal Corps to obtain permission to use the photograph. I gave them what little information I had in an attempt to credit the photographer. After several months of unsucessful attempts to identify the photographer, the Signal Corps conceded that it would be a nearly impossible task and they gave me permission to use the photo.

We do not know if that soldier survived the war or not. It is as though an angel of God appeared, accomplished a single purpose and then disappeared without a trace.

PREFACE

This is not a heavily researched documentary about Vietnam. It is not about injustices foisted upon our service men and women, nor is it any sort of political commentary with "pearls of wisdom" on how Americans could have done this, that, or the other. It is quite simply *my* story about *my* experiences in Vietnam. I never dwell on "could have" or "should have;" either you did, or you didn't. I went to Vietnam because I perceived it to be the right thing to do. I went as a very young man and returned a year older, somewhat wiser, and with some perspectives altered by the experience known as *war*.

I do not dwell on the horrors of war; plenty of other books do that. Rather, I focus on some of the more mundane human foibles of an average guy who was somehow protected from serious injury by a host of angels. Many of the people with whom I have crossed paths in my 56 years are aware of how great a miracle it is that I am even able to write this, let alone remember incidents and people from thirty-plus years ago.

My main purpose in writing this is to provide an account for the many sisters and mothers like my own who watched as their brothers or sons went off to war and who waited patiently and prayerfully for our safe return. Many did not come back, and those who waited in vain couldn't help wondering "How it must have been" or "How it would have been if..." A secondary purpose is to show that people can go to war and come back able to make a meaningful contribution to society. It also provides a different perspective for those who remember Vietnam as something reported on TV or portrayed at the movies.

These vignettes portray a less spectacular, human side of the war. My perspective is that error was both human and common place. If articles seem chaotic or out of sequence, that is a reflection of the kaleidoscopic nature of my experience. It was not a smooth, organized, well sequenced series of events. Vietnam veterans do not remember their tours in orderly, chronological sequences, but rather as chaotic sets of priority driven events. *I was shot down. I crashed. A friend was killed. The enemy blew up my base camp.*

Before I say much more, I want to point out a few things:

1. Vietnam was not a vacation; it was not full of fun and laughs;

2. I lost my best friend, Donney Kilpatrick, to the one and only round fired from an aged .51 caliber machine gun during an air assault. It hit him in the face;

3. I saw some horrible things during a year in Vietnam and had the task of medically evacuating scores of young Americans who probably did not survive. It was disheartening to see how many of those deaths and injuries were due to FFI (Failure to Follow Instructions). I also saw a number of Americans die, two of whom were in my platoon. It is beyond my ability to describe the sense of loss, futility, and intense sadness one suffers when that happens. I am also unable to describe what it does to you when you examine the people to whom you had just returned fire and

find one of them to be a young woman whose exposed breasts indicated a mother still nursing a baby.

4. A large number of Americans came away from Vietnam "warped" by what they had been through, and I am not trying to make light of their mental anguish or emotional scars. They are very real, and the healing process is arduous. It has only been in the last few years that I have been able to openly discuss even the lighter aspects of "my experience." I do not see it as a coincidence that my healing has taken place since I joined a church and got to know my Savior. I have been through too many close calls to attribute my survival to chance.

I kept my little "Platoon Leader's Notebook" from Vietnam. I have the names of each of the members of my platoon, the ones who made it and the three that did not. I left out names of anyone who I thought might have been embarrassed or hurt by what I wrote. All the names I mention here are real. They are real Americans—decent kids placed in the most difficult circumstance any human being can face. All of us were frightened and at times terrified fighting an enemy who hid in tall grass, spider holes, trees, and huts and was hard to identify. But we all stayed with it until our tours were over.

Ralph Waldo Emerson wrote, "A hero is no braver than the ordinary man, but he is braver just five minutes longer." My Vietnam was full of heroes: some were reluctant passengers hoping the pilots wouldn't do something stupid to kill everybody on board. Others were crew chiefs, door gunners, military policemen, nurses, fellow pilots, cooks, and radio operators from the control towers across Vietnam.

Many fathers, brothers, sisters, wives, and mothers who stayed at home waiting for our return were also heros. Some were little girls whose daddies never came back.

I notice that there are large gaps between what actually happened and what children are able to understand concerning their parents' experiences. (When Grandpa Finch died all that he had done and experienced was lost to all of us.) So I thought I'd write down a few "war stories" about my experiences in Vietnam. That way my children and grandchildren might have a *real* record of what I did in Vietnam.

Keep in mind that flying a helicopter requires the pilot to have both hands and both feet on the controls at all times. The pilot's eyes continuously scan all the instruments and about 20 gauges to monitor oil pressure, fuel, engine rpm, rotor rpm, and aircraft trim and balance. Additionally, he must look outside the aircraft from time to time to see where he is going and change heading altitude and air speed. The appendix discusses helicopters in more detail.

I reported to Cu Chi (pronounced *coo chee*) in January 1969 as a twenty-four year old Army helicopter pilot. If you find pictures of Lieutenant Finch, you will note that I didn't even look twenty. (I was forever being asked for ID when I tried to buy a beer.) The orders sending me to flight school and Vietnam are in my old trunk with the Army junk in it.

In Country

What was it like upon arrival in Vietnam? It wasn't so much frightening as it was confusing. I had been to the tropics before in the summers of 1963 and 1966 to visit my parents in Thailand. I thought I would be familiar with the assault on my senses: the smell of tropical humidity, fetid water, rotting things, tapioca drying in the sun, the oppressive heat and humidity. The atmosphere is somehow different in the tropics. It seems harder to breathe. There is also a sense of being some place really different. I had traveled with my family all over Europe and many of the States, places where people eat roughly the same things, smell roughly the same, and with the exception of language differences, act about the same. Vietnam was different. Not only was it tropical, but there was the added sense it was a hostile fire zone. Here, people were at war.

Arrival in Vietnam

My World Airways Boeing 707 left Travis Air Force Base near San Francisco at 0515, stopped in Honolulu to refuel, and landed at Tan Sohn Nuht Air Base just outside Saigon at about 1600 (4:00 P.M.) on a sunny afternoon in

January 1969. We had all heard that the Tet Offensive was in progress. All we really knew was that it meant the bad guys were attacking. We were all apprehensive. We were staring out the windows at "The War Zone," wondering what would happen to us next. Many of the guys on board feared they would not leave in one piece.

The aircraft taxied to a stop and they rolled a ramp over to the door. As soon as the door opened that tropical humidity rushed in. The air was hot, humid, tropical and thick with odors that assaulted our senses. I noticed some new smells mixing with the tropical odors: gun powder, JP-4 (jet fuel), both of which have a distinctive odor, and the acrid smell of something really disgusting. Later I found out it was poop.

We burned American poop in Vietnam. I'm not exactly sure why. Maybe we were scared a lot and didn't want everyone to know, or maybe we just ate too much mess hall food. Anyway, the poop was collected in large 55 gallon drums, doused with jet fuel and burned. It sent up great billows of black smoke with a disgusting smell that hung in the air for hours.

I sometimes get a whiff of jet fuel or gun powder and am instantly reminded of Vietnam.

I spent the first night in Long Binh at the personnel replacement Battalion, or "Ree Po Depot," with other "newbies" while they decided where I was to go and how they were to get me there. I received a whole bunch of jungle fatigues, boots, and my jungle hat. That night in the tropical heat I heard the distant thunder of artillery fire, and wondered what the next year would be like.

The next morning I listened to some of the guys complain about all sorts of things. I ate and tried to take a walk, but I was only allowed to walk around the compound. At about two o'clock someone called my name. I was assigned to the 25th Infantry Division base camp at Cu Chi, and told to get ready.

About an hour later, I was flown to Cu Chi in a helicopter belonging to my own company. I noted that we flew generally northwest for about half an hour. (That tidbit of information was useful a few days later when the North Vietnamese made an all out assault on Cu Chi.)

I was dropped off in a really dusty, open area with a distinctive smell and was told to walk over to "The Bear Pit." I had no idea what that meant, and wandered around for a few minutes before finding someone who pointed it out. Learning it was on the other side of the main runway, I made my way across, dodging between landing and departing aircraft, then through a series of huts constructed out of ammunition boxes.

The Little Bear

I was assigned to A company of the 25th Aviation Battalion. I was not very impressed. It was hot and there

Welcome to Little Bear Country

was dusty red clay everywhere I looked. The strips of red clay used for Jeep traffic were darkened by Kreosote and the whole place smelled like the telephone poles we had in the early 50's in Tucson.

I discovered the company mascot was a Japanese Sun bear. Each of our aircraft had a Little Bear painted on the nose and either side of the tail-boom The radio call sign was "Little Bear." The aircraft parking area consisting of one maintenance hanger for major repairs and an area of twenty-seven revetments or reinforced stalls for aircraft called "The Bear Pit." Our unit was part of the 25th Aviation Battalion which was assigned to the Twenty-Fifth Infantry Division whose patch was a stylized red taro leaf with a lightning bolt through it. We referred to it as the "Electric Strawberry."

A Company, B Company, a maintenance company and the Headquarters Company formed the 25th Aviation Battalion, the organic aviation units for the 25th Infantry Division, nicknamed the Tropic Lightning Division.

The Little Bears had a proud history before I arrived at Cu Chi in 1969. They were selected as the Aviation Unit of the Year and won a variety of unit awards for valor. The Little Bears grew out of the 175th Assault Helicoptor Co. which was formed at Ft. Benning, Georgia in 1965, as part

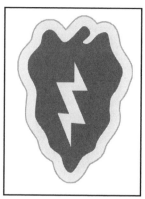

25th Infantry Division patch, known as the "Electric Strawberry"

*Unit patch, "A" Company
25th Aviation Battalion*

of the 11ᵗʰ Air Assault Brigade, an experimental unit formed at that time to test airmobility concepts.

The 25ᵗʰ Aviation Battalion was originally stationed with the division in Hawaii, but was light on aircraft assets. On the 14ᵗʰ of March, 1966, the 175ᵗʰ Assault Helicoptor Company left Ft. Benning by air for Oakland, CA. At Oakland, they boarded the troop ship, USNS *Upshur*, a reconditioned troop ship. One member of the battalion remembered crossing the Atlantic on this same ship. The ship left Oakland on the Ides of March, 1966, along with various other units bound for Vietnam. Enroute, the 175ᵗʰ Aviation Company was re-designated to "A" Company, 25ᵗʰ Aviation Battalion, 25ᵗʰ Infantry Division.

The commander of the 175ᵗʰ was asked what the call sign and unit name would be for the new unit. Major Earnest Elliot thought for a moment, and recalled a story his mother had read to him about an Indian in a cupboard who magically came to life to accomplish wonderful things. The Indian's name was Little Bear.

The *Upshur* dropped off accompanying units all along the coast of South Vietnam from Cam Rhan Bay to Vung Tau. The 25ᵗʰ Aviation Battalion disembarked at Vung Tau, a resort south of Saigon. There, they boarded C130 cargo planes for the ride to Ton Son Nhut airfield at Saigon. The 25ᵗʰ Aviation Battalion's own helicoptors, which had been shipped over earlier, transported the battalion from Ton Son

Nhut to their new home at Cu Chi, about 25 miles to the northwest. I was totally oblivious to all of that.

Our sister company, B company of the 25th Aviation Battalion was the Attack helicopter company and they had begun to receive the new AH-1 Cobra attack helicopters. They had painted shark teeth on the front of their aircraft to make them look even more forbidding. Their call sign was "Diamond Head."

The selection of the unit call sign and our mascot, Spooky, was done with methodical forethought and some degree of reverence. We didn't have much time to learn about a unit's history, we just accepted our assignments, dug in as soon as we were able, got a check-out on the local flying area, and went to war. It was a very busy time.

Before my arrival the Little Bears had moved from the lush paradise of Hawaii to that God-forsaken spot of clay marsh named Cu Chi. What a rude awakening that must have been. The first flight standardization and instructor pilot for A company after it's arrival in Vietnam was Major Robert "Spook" Grundman. Spook Grundman set the flight performance standards that we all followed. Spook was well-liked, and had been instrumental in finding and res-cuing from a hillside a baby Japanese sun bear, adopted as our unit mascot. When Major Grundman was shot down and killed on September 26, 1966, they named the little sun bear Spooky in his honor.

Spooky was a very personable little creature not much bigger than the average dog, but very strong. We used to give her little cartons of milk which she would hold in her paws, tip upwards to her muzzle, and drain with relish.

In that mode she was cute. But then the guys took to giving her cans of beer. They thought it was funny to see her sitting on her haunches drinking beer, so they kept giv-ing her more. Well, after about six to ten beers she started acting strange. A couple of times she tore open her cage and went on a rampage through the base camp. One time she went to the neighboring Field Artillery section, tore into the Commanding Officer's hooch, ripped the door off his refrigerator, and helped herself to everything edible. At times like that we had to round up a posse, hunt the poor thing down, rope her, and drag her back to her cage. She would sleep for a few hours and be back to normal. Of course everybody would apologize and promise not to get her drunk again. But they did anyway.

I remember one time I got back late and headed for my hooch with serious intent to sleep. I turned on the light in my room, and there was Spooky, sitting on my bed with the remnants of a package of grape Kool Aid all over everything. I had received some cookies in a cardboard box, and I guess the smell had brought her to my room. She had raided someone else's room first and brought the Kool Aid with her, ready to party. After digging through a couple of empty boxes in my room she was about partied out.

Usually her binges would end when she got very sleepy and just sort of crashed. This particular time she was still full of energy and when I startled her she went out through the nearest wall. She crashed right through the wall next to the window and kept on going.

When I left Vietnam she was still there and the guys were still feeding her candy, milk and an occasional beer.

Finding A Home

I managed to find the Commander's office and reported for duty. The C.O. was a crusty old Army Major who was out of patience for that day, and had not figured out how or where to work me into the unit. He directed me to the mess hall to look for a Lieutenant Hinson who was to be my Platoon Leader. I was also told to get some rest. No one bothered to mention *where* I was to get some rest, but the Platoon Leader eventually found me a place to spend the night.

I was introduced to a Warrant Officer who would be leaving the next day on a "Freedom Bird" to go back to the States. Our company area was a series of wooden shacks built out of empty wooden ammunition boxes with corrugated tin roofs and sand bags about three feet high around the outside. Each hooch had two to four rooms. Some were named and had signs to provide comic relief from the reality of where we were: a war zone. These "hooches" were linked by a series of wooden walkways which I was to find invaluable during the rainy season. I was informed that it was"the sys- tem" to buy your "hooch" from someone who was leaving.

Three guys happened to be leaving over the next few days, so I talked to each of them and found a reasonable deal. I paid $50 for a hooch not too far from the "three holer." (One of our outhouses was a luxury model with three holes

Lt. Finch in front of hooch

Cu Chi's Holiday Inn (a hooch with a sign for comic relief)

in a plank over three 55 gal. drums cut in half.) The deal included a packet of all the maps I would probably need during my one year stay and a fan. Nice touch.

I never had a single regret about buying my hooch. It kept me dry during monsoons, wind and thunderstorms. It was also a whole lot better than what the Infantry had out in the mud. I was not aware that some of the guys had air conditioners and even "bunkers" (hiding places reinforced with bags of dirt built into their "hooches"). I was happy to have found a place quickly. The fan would have cost $20 by itself. Most importantly, I had arrived!

At night, lying there listening to the sound of distant artillery, you couldn't help but wonder where you would fit in, how you could earn your "wings," and whether you would make it through a year of war. At times, I felt like a kid who was a long way from Tucson. It wasn't fear really, more like loneliness. I remember thinking I should go to sleep exhausted every night so I would not ponder the imponderables too much.

A surprise bonus came the second day when I came "home" and found my boots spit shined and all my clothes cleaned and stacked neatly on a freshly made bunk! The place came with maid service! We paid the "hooch maids" something like $10 per month. The services included laundry, daily spit-shining of boots, as well as dusting and cleaning on mornings after a mortar attack. She would also give free lessons in Vietnamese, and periodically did special jobs like sewing on name tags and minor repairs to uniforms.

We all learned a couple of Vietnamese words: *Trung We* was Lieutenant, *Dai We* was Captain, *Dinky Dau* was crazy, and I was called that more than once. "Numbah One" meant the best or first quality, and *Dee Dee Muah* (from the French, *Dite Mois*, or "speak to me" used when a French person answers the phone) meant the phone or sometimes the radio. *Dee dee mao* meant high tail it out of there fast!

With my natural affinity for languages, I should have been able to learn more Vietnamese, but I was pretty busy. I never became conversant in Vietnamese.

The next day my Platoon Leader sent me to Survival

Laundry set out to dry

School. For ten days we learned all the nasty things the North Vietnamese could do to us, and how they "booby trapped" things. "So don't touch any weapons you see lying around...etc."

They also put us all on "the pill," a large yellow pill and a small white one to be taken every day we were assigned to Vietnam. They were anti-malaria and anti-dysentery pills. For the first few days after starting on those horse pills I couldn't go to the bathroom at all. I felt like I had been corked shut! However, many of the lessons from that survival school were good and I have continued to use them.

One of those is the use of peripheral vision to see at night. If you look straight at something, you are using a less sensitive portion of your eye. If you scan around you can pick out much fainter light sources with "the side of your eyesight."

I learned about the curious "tattle tale weeds," a small fern-like plant which grew like grass in large patches of ground, but had a curious trait. If touched, it would fold its leaves and shrink away for about thirty minutes. So, if someone or a group of people walked through it, there would be a trail of folded leaves for about thirty minutes. Then they would spread out again.

Another thing we learned in the jungle survival school was that there was a price on our heads. Second Lieutenants were worth $500! Captains were worth $1000! Pilots, I'll never forget, were worth $10,000, just for the head! (If they brought in my whole body I suppose there would be a bonus?) That would have been a lot of money for me, let alone a Vietnamese soldier who was lucky to get a month's ration of rice. So, they had ample incentive to try to get me! Every time we started receiving fire, I remembered *"Ten Thousand Dollar Reward!"* I thought to myself, "That poor starving devil is trying to get my scalp so he can collect a reward!" (I think that is when I started smoking.)

There were a number of lessons taught at survival

school which could have prevented many of the injuries I was to see later as I evacuated wounded American soldiers. Many had failed to listen or had forgotten those lessons.

After survival school, I went about the business of getting back into a cockpit in my new company. Cu Chi was considered a "Base Camp" and had all the amenities of home, there was a Post Exchange or PX where we could buy a variety of goods including stereo sound systems, circulating fans, watches, cigarettes, magazines, and other such items. The PX also had a photo development counter, a massage parlor and a Barber Shop! Real troops, like the line artillery and infantry battalions usually had someone who was trained as a barber or even though not trained formally, was given license to shave heads and butcher hair in the war zone.

At Cu Chi we were more civilized than that. We were, after all, a Base Camp and other units went to Cu Chi to take a rest and relaxation or "R and R" break from the

As a First Lieutenant and pilot, my head was worth $10,000

war, buy a few beers and sit down without being shot at for a day or two.

After several weeks, I made my first trip to the PX. I was accustomed to PX's in the states, so being in need of toiletries, soap, and a few goodies, I went to the PX and thought I'd spruce up my appearance with a hair cut while I was at it. I walked into the barbershop and noticed that the barbers were all oriental looking folks. Men's haircuts can be done quite well using just an electric razor, comb and scissors, so I didn't think much more about it. I sat down to wait my turn, which was right quick.

As I was staring at myself in the mirror I studied the guy giving me a haircut and it dawned on me that they were Vietnamese. Here we were out shooting at these folks, and they or their relatives had been shooting back at us, now I found myself in a chair with a linen around my neck at the mercy of this guy who could very well have been a North Vietnamese Army soldier hiding out and gathering intelligence information about the GI's at Cu Chi.

When he brought out a straight razor, stropped it few times to show me it was sharp and proceeded to pull my ears nice and taught. I had to swallow hard. It would have been so easy for him to slice off my ears or simply slit my throat! Egads! I tried to comfort myself with the idea he would not get very far away before someone would catch him, and he would loose his job!! What!? Who would care about the fifty dollar a day job if he could show he slit the throat of an American pilot and collect the $10,000 reward? I did not make many trips to the barber shop.

One of my trips to the PX became a somber event. As I walked towards the PX, I saw a tall officer with a cane and bandages. He looked somewhat familiar so I looked at him more closely, then realized it was Andrew M___. We had been in Infantry Officer Candidate School together. Andy was one of those men that just looks handsome. He was tall, muscular, well proportioned, had a good complexion, with an almost majestic gait, was clean cut, lean, square jawed and downright good looking.

In OCS he had earned a reputation as a bonifide asshole. He always had to have things his way. He tattled on people if they brought in candy or pogey bait, reported people for smoking after lights out, was ruthless and harsh when he held leadership positions and he was often mean spirited with the rest of us. He always had to be right and the only one whose opinion was valid; but, the worst thing was his obsession that he have things his way and only his way.

Andy went more or less directly to Vietnam while I became first a training officer at Fort Rucker and then attended flight school. So, his tour was over. He was getting ready to return to the United States and I had only been there a matter of weeks. Andy had been shot up pretty bad, one leg seemed to be shorter than the other, he was somehow bent sideways from the waist up, and one arm was withered badly. I chatted with him a little to catch up on where he had been since OCS, and asked about his wounds. He told me that he had led a charge up a hill into enemy fire, had received seven nearly fatal wounds, and had been submitted for a Medal of Honor.

I was stunned into silence. I listened to his tale for a while. He said he had to catch up with his friends and hobbled off, leaving me in front of the PX.

One of our senior Warrant Officer pilots, Pat Lawlor, came up and asked me what Andy had to say, so I explained that we had been classmates and related what he had told me.

Mr. Lawlor said, "That officer was shot by his own men!"

His troops hated him something fierce. One day he pushed them too far. He tried to get his men to charge a machine gun emplacement when it really wasn't necessary. They told him it would be suicide, asked him to call for air support or a helicopter gunship to hit the emplacement. He refused, turned on his "my-way-or-nothing" charm and ordered people to assault the machine gun nest. The troops initially did what he said, but two or three of them were pinned down by enemy fire and one was hit. Then the non-commissioned officers rebelled. When he went up to push the men forward, his own troops shot him with 2 magazines of M-16 rounds.

One of those rounds went in through his back, hit his lung, tore the muscles on his right side, and gave him that twisted stance. Two rounds hit his femur and shattered it so badly they had to cut a chunk of it out. He was medically evacuated all right, and survived near fatal wounds, but there was no medal of honor waiting for him.

Going Potty In Vietnam

You may be wondering why I would even write about this! But let me assure you that it was as different as everything else in RVN. Most Americans grow up with a flushing toilet and have never seen a real outhouse. Outhouses are a part of our American heritage which is being forgotten amidst all the changes brought about in the Twentieth Century. But, not too long ago, all Americans had to use an outhouse. Generally they were little wooden shacks with a holed bench sitting over a hole in the ground. Little piles of paper placed within convenient reach served as toilet paper. (Even further back there was a ditty, "wiped their arse on blades of grass and walked away contented.") What you know of as toilet paper, is a relatively new twist for a very old need.

In Vietnam we had outhouses. They were a shock to most of us with all these piles of newspaper and 55 gallon drums to collect the daily excrement. So, I like everyone else, was indoctrinated on "proper outhouse etiquette." It's the pits to get to the outhouse in a big hurry, plop down and then realize there was no paper! So you always took some paper with you to restock the place. From time to time we had a real treat when someone brought real toilet paper from the States. Imagine: getting excited about toilet paper.

Showers were primitive too. Ours had a huge tank which had been the external fuel pod from a big airplane on the roof of the shower room. It collected rain water, got some water from the mess hall, and was heated mainly by sunshine. The first shower of the evening was fairly warm, but by morning the water had cooled off considerably making showers rather brisk.

Those two niceties of life being absent in the War Zone, when guys got a chance to take a vacation, (normally ten days off for "R&R"—rest and recuperation), they acted very strange around bathrooms. By force of habit they always found some way to take in a newspaper. They would often flush the toilet repeatedly just to watch the water swirl around and around taking everything with it. And they became notorious shower hogs, spending twenty minutes or more in a hot shower. In Vietnam neither the shower nor the outhouse were safe.

We had a red-headed Irish Warrant Officer by the name of Jeff O'Hara who was literally caught with his pants down during a mortar attack. Jeff looked rather like Yosemite Sam, that cartoon character who always shoots at Bugs Bunny. He had one of those magnificent mustaches that curl out and up ending in a spiraling point. Even his voice rather matched that of the cartoon character.

Well, Jeff was on the "john" when the first few mortar rounds of a daylight attack came in, and seeing as how it was broad daylight, he elected to stay put.

The normal pattern for daylight attacks was for them to shoot a few rounds and quit. It was called "harassing fire." It was designed to keep us confused and immobilized for a few moments.

So Jeff sat. The very next round was a "122" (122 millimeter rocket) which hit just behind the crapper and made a heck of a mess. It blew the 55 gallon drum of poop high enough to slam into the bottom of the bench with the holes cut in it where Jeff was sitting, splattering its contents all over him. Boy! He came out of there in a hurry all covered with crap, trying to run with his pants down around his knees and cursing up a storm.

He was not hurt, which was a minor miracle, but his pride and ego were in torment. I can still see Jeff trying to run with his pants down around his thighs, poop all over him and that majestic mustache veritably dripping with shit! Lord! He had a right to be angry. To make matters worse, five or six of us were watching his antics and laughing—more with him than at him, but we *were* laughing, and that didn't help Jeff's condition. I do hope he forgave us.

Becoming a Little Bear

A Company, The Little Bears, flew "Slicks," meaning that there were no rocket pods hanging off the sides of the aircraft, no cannon or minigun pods hanging off the bottom or the nose of the aircraft. The sides of the Little Bear aircraft were clean or slick.

B Company, The Diamond Heads, flew "Guns" and Loaches. They started with "B," or Bravo model, later upgraded to "C," or Charlie model, Hueys with rocket pods on the sides and some were configured with machinegun or cannon pods under the nose. Eventually, in 1968 and 1969, they transitioned to the AH-IG Cobra gunships. The gunships formed hunter killer teams with a Light Observation Helicoptor, or LOH, pronounnced Loach. The LOH drivers were truly crazy pilots. Their mission was to fly low and slow over the enemy, draw their fire, pinpoint the enemy locations and call the gunships for help. The Gunships simply rolled in to shoot the targets. The LOH pilots got shot at *all the time*. It was their mission in life to get shot at. Live bait! What kind of a person would take on that job willingly?

The mission of the Diamond Heads was straightforward: Find and shoot the enemy, provide Aerial Rocket Artillery, and close-in fire support to the Infantry.

Little Bear 628

The mission of the Little Bears was less clearly defined. The third platoon of the Little Bears flew VIP's. The first and second platoons flew "Ash and Trash," or General Support. The types of mission varied based on what the ground units needed. Little Bears flew troop lift missions, resupply of ammunition and food, mail and courier missions, replacement missions taking communication security equipment to the line units, and bus and taxi service for the 25th Infantry Division. We took the less important people hither and thither across the III Corps area of South Vietnam. We had one other mission we all liked to support. We performed "test bed" missions where we experimented with various applications of the helicopter, including one developed during 1969, that became known as the Nighthawk.

To become proficient as a Diamond Head you had to learn to find and shoot targets. How were we supposed to become proficient as Little Bears?

For three or four days after I finished Jungle school, I asked for a "local area orientation," but either no one was available or there were no aircraft. The standardization officer, and Instructor pilot, Ed Behne, had to give you a checkride before you could be allowed to fly in country. Ed was busy so I had to wait.

I hadn't flown since Flight School, and was quickly forgetting critical skills, so I started bugging everyone at the flight line. Finally one guy in my platoon who was finished with his missions for that day gave me a quick fifteen minute ride around the traffic pattern.

I was all eyeballs. I didn't pick up which frequencies to use for local traffic because everything was on "pre-sets" and you couldn't read the frequencies (kind of like a pre-set frequency on a car radio, but without the digital read-out). But I did see the little village just to the northwest of our base camp, and got an appreciation for the size of Cu Chi.

It was an Air Force base and an Army base combined,

Aerial view of Cu Chi

with all kinds of Artillery units, Military Police (MP's), the 25th Infantry Division headquarters, all in one big circle surrounded with barbed wire and machine-gun positions around the perimeter. Everything was a red clay dirt except for a few roads that were covered with oil. Other people in Vietnam could always distinguish those of us who were assigned to Cu Chi because we always had this red clay dust on us. I had heard the Artillery fire at night, and it was loud. From the air I could see why; the Howitzers were fairly close to our company area.

Baptism By Fire

Two nights later, February 26th, 1969 at about 2200 hrs., all hell broke loose. We were under a major attack. For a new guy, or FNG (F—ing New Guy), it was a major ordeal.

First, a few machine guns were heard on the perimeter, then lots of machine gun and small arms fire, then a whole lot of incoming mortars, rockets, and artillery came crashing down all around us. The perimeter went nuts! Everybody who had anything was shooting it! There were bullets and little pieces of hot metal called shrapnel zinging all around the place.

I still have a "Bic" pen which had been on my night stand. It was hit by shrapnel still hot enough to fuse the plastic and ink together and knock the pen up against the wall.

Guys were hollering and hooting and running every which way. People kept telling me to get down, get up and move, get under cover, and to do this or that—all at the same time of course. It's never like they give you a choice. It's not like the movies either where three or four "cool" guys give a few curt orders and the bad guys take it in the shorts. Panic was everywhere!

I thought to myself, "Enough of this! Let me out of here!" Helmet in hand, I ran to Operations and found our

"Fearless Operations Officer" hiding under the Flight Operations desk. I asked him which aircraft I could take to evacuate at least one of them. He peeked out from under the desk with his steel pot on and informed me that I was a total idiot because, "Charlie had broken through the wire," but if I wanted to be a lunatic, I could take "123" which was parked in the second revetment in the Bear Pit.

At that point I wasn't really sure what they meant by "broke through the wire," but it didn't sound like good news! I said "OK," looked down at my feet, noticed I had on flip-flop thongs and an old gray flight suit, but, what the heck, I sure didn't want to stay there! Mind you, it was dark and I wasn't all that familiar with our company area even in daylight.

I ran the hundred yards to the Bear Pit, flip flops slapping against my feet, found the aircraft in the dark and started to preflight it.

Preflight is tough to do at night in the dark, especially when you are in a big hurry. As I remember it, there were a few parachute flares to help me see what I was doing. Shells seemed to be falling all over the place, and all the machine-gun, artillery, and incoming fire made a heck of a noise. I did not conduct a textbook preflight inspection, and did not climb up on top to check tolerances in the various nuts, blades and push rods. I did untie the main rotor blade and take off the cowling covers, so I knew I could get it started, but I had never tried a take-off out of one of those revetments and was sure that would be a challenge.

In Vietnam we parked our aircraft in stalls somewhat like horse stalls with reinforced steel walls to minimize damage from stray bullets and shrapnel while we were under attack. The aircraft fit in those stalls with about three feet of clearance on each side. The guy who gave me the orientation ride told me that the Operations Officer had crashed one of our aircraft trying to get out of the revetment during *daylight*.

Just as I was beginning to worry about whether I had tackled a project well beyond my level of competence, there was this tremendous explosion behind me and a flash of fire bright enough to make shadows. So, what would you do?

I jumped into the cockpit and started the aircraft as best as I could from memory. I had left the log book and checklist in operations, but everything seemed to be going just fine. The engine sounded right as the primary and secondary turbines kicked in. The blades started to turn. Next, I saw these shadows in the darkness running and jumping onto the aircraft, and then I was overwhelmed by tear gas. I couldn't remember how to get the landing lights turned on. I couldn't see the instrument gauges to tell if the rotor RPM was high enough to fly with. I kept blinking through the tear gas with my face six inches from the instrument panel trying to find out what the hell the aircraft was doing. Someone in the back yelled that we should get going. He had no idea how relieved I was to discover that the guys who jumped on spoke English! Then someone climbed into the left front seat. I asked him if he was a pilot. He said, "Yes!"

I said, "Good! Get the damned landing lights on and let's get out of here!"

"I don't remember where they are," he said, "but I think they're on *your* side. I hope you know what you're doing. I just got here from the States, and don't know my way around!"

"Oh Great! Me too," I said. "Strap yourself in. I'm pulling pitch."

I pulled up on the collective to bring us to a hover. As we started to clear the ground, two or three more people jumped on. I was afraid I would hit the side of the revetment, so I pulled it up very slow, blinking through the tear gas till we were clear on both sides at about a ten foot hover, then pulled all the way up to almost fifty pounds of torque. (You only need about eighteen to twenty pounds of torque to take off normally.) We went straight up for awhile, then the other pilot cleared his eyes long enough to tell me we were flying *backwards* at a fairly good clip. What the heck! At least we were flying and that seemed preferable to whatever was going on below.

The good news was that we were at nearly a thousand feet and clear of all the gas. So what if we were flying backwards? We were alive and well, breathing fresh air again and *flying*. However, we were lost without radio communication. Neither of us knew what radio frequency to use to tell Little Bear Ops. (Operations) that we were airborne and OK, nor what frequency to use so we could ask Cu Chi Tower for departure instructions for permission to take off. Not that it really mattered anymore. We were airborne!

The scene below was nasty with large fires everywhere, multiple explosions from the west side of the base, and quite a few aircraft on fire. We knew we weren't going back right away. I leveled off and headed south, remembering that we had flown more or less north to get to Cu Chi.

We decided to risk seeming foolish in order to stay alive, so we turned on the radio and tuned in the International Emergency Frequency, 243.0KHZ. One of us had to make the announcement, and I had already done enough silly things for one night, so I asked my co-pilot (I think his name was Jim) to make the call.

"Mayday, Mayday! Any station! This is...(What the hell is our number anyway?)...OK, Little Bear 123. We are airborne and lost somewhere over Cu Chi. Request assistance. Over!"

My, my! But that got a response!

"Aircraft 123, you said 'Mayday' and you are airborne. What's the problem?"

"Hey! Are you guys nuts? Whadd'ya mean you're over

Cu Chi and you're lost? Which one is it?"

"Call sign 123, you are on Guard Radio" (meaning the emergency channel) "Change frequency to..." (I'm not sure what frequency they gave us, but we did it gladly!)

"Did you say 'Little Bear?' If so go to 47.5 on your Fox Mike (which meant the FM radio) and contact Ops for instructions!"

You can imagine all the harassing comments all those pilots and tower controllers were making about us inside their respective cockpits and towers. A lot of folks had a good laugh at our expense, but we got out of there alive and well.

Anyhow, now we were organized. I talked to Operations on the FM radio and was given frequencies to use, and was told to take the aircraft to Long Binh and stay the night. Jim contacted Cu Chi tower, explained the situation, got frequencies for our flight to Long Binh, and even contacted another Little Bear who was airborne and gave us vectors to Long Binh. ("Vectors" are directions determining the position of one point relative to another.)

Then we realized we were going to land soon and had about fifteen minutes to figure out how to get the damned light on. Neither of us was going to ask for help on that one. You know, it's amazing how many switches there are on a helicopter! We tried them *all* that night. Little Bear 248 was kind enough to fly around in circles waiting for us over Long Binh, although we had a devil of a time finding one blinking red light against the backdrop of a large city.

At that point my pilot skills were not sharp enough to realize that all we had to do was drop down a little and the other aircraft would have been easy to spot against the backdrop of a black tropical night sky. In an aircraft, whatever is below you is *below* your apparent horizon, and whatever is above you is *above* your apparent horizon. So if you loose a little altitude in relation to another aircraft, it pops up above your horizon. In a commercial jet, as you look out the window, whatever is on the horizon is at the same altitude as the aircraft you are riding in.

Eventually we located our sister ship and followed her into the heliport at Long Binh. When we finally landed we counted eight other guys on our aircraft. All safe.

To our surprise we found other Little Bear pilots at Long Binh too in various states of undress. A big Cajun Warrant Officer named Randy Juge had run out with his helmet, skivvy shorts, zories and a large knife! (He never went anywhere without that knife.) He lifted off just about the time I got permission to take 123, so he had missed all the tear gas and thought our story about flying blind was pretty funny. But, he was quick to point out that *we had made it,* and conceded we had done pretty good for a couple of FNG's. As we went to sleep that night you could see fire on the horizon. It was Cu Chi!

I slept fitfully. The next morning we went to get chow

A Chinook on approach

and were informed that they didn't have any extra chow for a bunch of pilots. I do not remember the details, but WO Juge offered to tear the place apart and eat anyway, or they could let us eat civil-like at tables and all that, and we would leave their mess hall intact. After a big breakfast with bacon and eggs and all the good stuff, we flew back to the devastation.

All the fuel and ammunition had been blown up. All the Chinooks were burned to the ground. Sappers, human bombs, with explosives strapped to their bodies ran into the aircarft and blew themselves up with the aircraft. After the explosion and fire from the burning fuel, there wasn't much left of the Chinook helicopters. All you could see were the main rotor hubs and the engines lying on the ground where they had fallen as the airframe burned away their structural support.

Procedures and an Orientation

You might think that after an initiation like that I would have learned enough about procedures for flying in Vietnam that I wouldn't need any further indoctrination. That is not the case. I made it through that by the skin of my teeth, and had quite a bit more to learn before I was entrusted with the responsibility for an aircraft, or as would happen later in my tour, be assigned a position as Platoon Leader, responsible for an airfield lighting system, nine aircraft, and the thirty-six crewmen to fly and maintain them. I was soon to find out Flight School barely qualified me to fly in a safe area. Learning the skills I would need to survive a year in Vietnam had just begun.

In Flight School we were taught radio procedures using standard Federal Aviation Agency (FAA) Rules. Normal codes for certain things were taken right out of the books. In Vietnam we had to learn a whole new set of procedures which we modified to suit our needs. Much of the change was designed to thwart the bad guys whom, by 1969, were monitoring a lot of our radio conversations.

Our codes became quite esoteric. The first time someone told me to "go up a golden anniversary and drop a nickel" I was totally confused. What he meant was add 50 kilohertz to the radio frequency I was using and subtract 5 kilohertz from the result. So, if I was at 35.0 on the FM radio, I was to re-tune the radio to 80.0 KHZ.

One of the least effective conventions, but one which stuck, was the use of numbers to identify rank or position. Six always referred to the commander. The Platoon Commander for the second platoon of A Company, twenty second Wolf Hounds might be, "Wolf Hound Alpha Two Six." The Commander for the Wolf Hounds would be "Wolf Hound Six." The Division Commander was "Tropic Lightning Six." For tactical reasons we were always taught to keep the transmissions short, concise and to the point, but we didn't.

There was always a lot of radio chatter, including the use of rather unorthodox procedures. For example, when you finish a radio call you are supposed to say, "Over," which means something like, "I finished what I had to say, now it's your turn." If you happen to be the one who initiated the call, you could say "Out," which means, "This is the end of the conversation." I heard a lot of people use "Roger, Dodger. Over and Out." Even the tower operators who were strictly trained by the FAA corrupted proper radio procedures with odd little names. One of the tower operators at Cu Chi adopted the fanciful personal call sign, "Electric Banana." We also had this cryptic code, "QNE" (pronounced "cue en eee"), which we used to signal our intent to change frequencies and terminate conversations with a station. For example, if I was leaving the Cu Chi airfield en route to Tay Ninh where I would spend the rest of the day, the conversation might be:

"Cu Chi tower, this is Little Bear 348. Request a straight out departure to the North. Over."

"Little Bear 348, this is Cu Chi Tower. You are cleared for straight out departure North. Call clear." *(Meaning report when you were clear of the traffic pattern.)*

"Roger Cu Chi Tower. 348 is clear and breaking north. QNE Thanks for your assistance. Have a nice day." *(That's short, concise, and to the point, isn't it?)*

"Roger 348. Frequency change approved. Watch out for the Chicken Man. The Electric Banana wishes you a good day. Cu Chi Tower out."

"Chicken Man?" The first time I heard that was when I was listening to the Armed Forces Network (AFN) broadcasting from Saigon. It was a radio station and if we were in no particular danger, we tuned the Automatic Direction finding radio to AFN. Sometimes, even if we were in danger, we had AFN on. That gave us a needle pointing to Saigon as a frame of reference for where we *were*, and allowed us to listen to music as we flew.

There was a lunatic disc jockey who told stories about a fictional character named Chicken Man and punctuated his stories with this horrible yell. "Chick—en Maaaaaan!" He had a unique call something like Tarzan's yodel, and lots of people tried to copy it. Anyway, here we were flying around in a combat zone, navigating by using the local rock and roll station, and laughing at this ridiculous Chicken Man screaming his head off on the radio. Is that any way to fight a war?

Seat designation in the aircraft was different from Flight School also. In a helicopter, most of the flight controls are duplicated on the left and right side of the cockpit. However, there are a few things which are more accessible from the right seat, and in Flight School we were being taught to be able to fly from the left seat. The instructor usually sat in the right seat. In Vietnam the senior seat was the left. The Aircraft Commander flew in the left seat with the pilot on the right. Additionally, in Flight School we had no gunners.

In Vietnam, the Crew Chief sat in the right rear seat armed with a 7.62 milimeter M-60 machine-gun with which he was vaguely familiar. The Crew Chief's forte was taking care of the aircraft, maintaining it and having it ready for the mission on time. Crew chiefs were amazing in the detail they knew about their aircraft. If something broke, they would often get it fixed overnight. Army crewchiefs were assigned to an aircraft whenever possible. Often, as that aircraft developed a history of rescuing people, successful Med Evac's or KIA's, the Crew Chief identified with *his* ship, bragged about it, praised it, talked to it and communed with the ship as if it were a living thing.

The gunner sat in the left rear seat with another M-60 machine-gun. But the guys selected to be gunners on our helicopters were *very* good Infantry Gunners who had spent

Cockpit: Enroute to Hotel 3

six months on the ground. The 25th Division was, after all, an Infantry Division. We should have been able to find some good gunners!

They knew a lot about where "Charlie" could hide, and had an instinct about where hostile fire was coming from. They generally had earned a reputation as good machine gunners, had good eyesight and were a cut above in all respects. They learned to anticipate locations where the enemy would likely be able to shoot at us. That is a very complex set of three-dimensional visual skills. As the aircraft climbs to altitude, trees and hedgerows shrink and the gaps between objects and trees seem to shrink. As we turn left or right, the tree lines would change aspect. A good gunner would anticipate the shrinkage along our flight path and visualize gaps that might appear as we passed woodlines. At 1500 feet human beings are very tiny targets. You can't tell much about them. Good gunners had a sixth sense for detecting hiding places. If someone did start to shoot at us, sharp gunners would be able to return fire almost immediately forcing the enemy to hide and suppressing the ground fire.

One of our gunners was a young black sergeant by the name of William Kenneth Hunter, big smile when he was happy and deadly serious when he was on the job, he seemed to know where people were going to shoot from before they fired the first shot. He became an expert at returning gunfire from a moving helicopter. If we were moving forward at 60 to 80 knots, you had to lead the target quite a bit, and if we were orbiting a fire fight, you had to do something else. I remember that he was exceptionally good. A good gunner like Sergeant Hunter could keep us all alive. And he did so more than once.

In May or June 1969, I was flying on a re-supply or ash and trash mission. We were flying Northwest towards Nui Ba Den when we received ground fire. Three distinct

"Crack's," and I could feel in my seat that something had struck the aircraft.

I heard the aircraft commander say, "Gunner! We're receiving fire from 9 o'clock low. Return fire!"

The gunner identified a target and opened up on him. "I got him sir!"

The ground fire quit. There were several other aircraft in the area, so we decided to go down to check out the ground situation. In between a couple of hooches our assailant was lying on the dirt road motionless.

There was a hunter-killer team orbiting us, a "scout" in a light observation helicopter and his big brother in a Cobra. We imagined we were pretty safe walking around with that brother watching over us. The gunner and I went over to see if our assailant had been a North Vietnamese Regular with a uniform and papers, or a Viet Cong soldier. I was watching the hooches for any sign of movement, nervous as a cat eating the dog's food.

I thought I was ready for anything, a hunter-killer team watching from above, an experienced machine-gunner next to me, a crew chief with a machine-gun trained on the hooches, and my M-16 at the ready. We approached the body in the road cautiously, the gunner told me to be careful that the person could have pulled the pin on a grenade that would explode as soon as the body was moved.

Nothing could prepare me for what was next. The gunner kept his body at a slant ready to run, jump back, duck or shoot, kicked the body's right leg to turn it over. It turned over easily enough, and both arms laid out flat to the sides, shirt top oozing blood. The face was so young and delicate. This couldn't be an NVA regular.

The gunner bent down to examine the body, tore open the shirt top. The chest was oozing blood from three M-60 machinegun wounds across the swollen breasts of a young girl. She couldn't have been more than 18 years old. Her breasts and nipples were enlarged. She had been breast feeding a baby!

You never know how you will react to such a violent, shocking scene. I didn't puke, though for a moment I thought I might. I held myself together fairly well till we got to the aircraft, then my legs started shaking uncontrollably. I don't think it was fear. Maybe disgust. Nerves? I was unable to fly the aircraft for a few minutes and the aircraft commander was kind enough to do all the flying and not mention it. No one will ever know what possessed that young girl to go out and shoot at an American helicopter.

The 25th Division area of operations bordered the Ocean to the East, and Cambodia to the West. Our sector of the Cambodian border stretched Northwest from an area called the Parrot's Beak in the South, at UTM grid coordinate X53092, past a central section called the Angel's Wing, and up to a portion alternatively called the Dog's Head or the Elephant's Ear in the Northwestern most section of the U.S. Army's III Corps area.

How many lives, how much ordinance did we expend along the Angel's Wing, and how many U.S. troops were wounded or killed there? Heaven knows. I can not remember how many people we evacuated from the patrol bases around the Angel's Wing, but quite a few.

On April 5, 1969, fierce fighting broke out at 01:30 at Fire base Diamond II, near the "Angel's Wing." It was a big enough event to make the Stars and Stripes and everyone in the Division knew something big was going on at the Angel's Wing.

I went as a pilot flying a flare ship. We dropped flares to light the scene below for four or five hours. When we ran out of flares, we raced back to Tay Ninh for a re-supply and came right back out. Helicopter gunships churned up the ground, Airforce fighters dropped bombs and rockets, ground forces of the 27th Wolfhounds called for artillery and mortar fire and we shot everything the 25th Division had available into that area.

The only chance we had to relieve ourselves was to pee off to the side of the ship while we were refueling or rearming. Sometimes the NCO's at the re-arm point would have a cup of coffee we could share, but it was a really long night.

Throughout the night, gunships came and went to re-arm and refuel. Who knows how many close calls we had as aircraft raced in and out of the contact area under the trajectory of all that artillery? One night another aircraft's luck ran out. As they were flying at 1500 feet, a 4.2 inch mortar round on the way to its intended target hit the top of a Huey in mid-air, exploding, killing everyone on board.

The aircraft commander on that flight was a light observation helicopter (LOH) pilot from the Diamond Heads who had not flown a night mission in Vietnam within the preceeding eight months. The pilot, WO-1 Mel Grant, had flown with Ed Mitchel earlier that day. Ed had recommended Mel for Aircraft Commander, and he would have taken his checkride the next day. Mel was considered by most of the unit pilots to be unusually proficient and well-qualified even though he had been in the country only a few months.

We watched over the course of the night as our forces took a beating. We heard reports of enemy soldiers being killed too, but that was hard to see at night.

Towards dawn the enemy pulled out and high-tailed it across the border to their sanctuary in Cambodia. The really sad part about that was that we were not allowed to cross the border into Cambodia to chase them. So they would get a good day's sleep and rest while our guys would have to continue on guard.

Many of us had seen a Cambodian sanctuary from the air, corrugated tin Quonset huts shining in the sun-

light, a motor pool full of jeeps and light trucks, a training
center and athletic fields. It really was a sanctuary and some
American politician had agreed that we would not go shoot
the enemy once they got there.

It was really President Lyndon Johnson's policy at
that time that kept us out of Cambodia. I am sure senior
military people advised the president of our plight. But,
LBJ did not budge.

I did get angry enough to hatch a half-assed plan for
revenge that night and we executed it a few weeks later.
When day light came and we began evacuating the wounded
it was clear that a lot of enemy soldiers died too. We picked
up wounded in three different lifts that day; I think we pulled
out 25. Bloody trails off into the jungle showed the Vietnamese had suffered significant losses. There were no
Medevacs for the enemy. No helicopters, no evacuation
hospital, no donut dollies. When they were wounded, they
were unceremoniously dragged off the field and not allowed
to make a sound. I wonder if they knew in advance that
they would get no help if they were in trouble. What made
them endure such hardship?

In May 1969, a Mechanized Battalion convoy with
about 15 Armored Personnel Carriers, was headed north
from Phouc Hoa when they ran into a well planned ambush about 5 miles East of Nui Ba Den. I was flying right
seat (pilot) as we went to offer assistance.

The brutal scene enacted below us was burned into my
memory. Their lead vehicles had tripped the ambush and
were immobilized in the middle of a narrow dirt road. One
was off to the left with the tracks blown off, another canted
to the right. The one in the center that had taken the brunt
of a land mine, was opened like a tin can. It was smoking
from whatever had caught fire inside of it. The ground on
each side of the road was soft mud. The three disabled
vehicles made a substantial obstacle. All the radio transmis-

sions were hard to understand because casualties near the man with the radio were screaming in pain and yelling louder than the man on the radio trying to talk to us.

They wanted Medevacs but were under such intense enemy fire we could not get in, so we circled helplessly above that mess for what seemed like an hour. The battalion commander was wounded, the Executive officer, a really young Major, took over and tried to maneuver one of the tracks around the obstacles, only to get the vehicle stuck in soft mud long enough to get hit with an RPG that stopped them dead. Several of the men on that track were wounded.

One of the Company commanders, a captain, took over as the acting Battalion commander and seemed to be making some headway organizing forward motion and training fire on some of the enemy positions. His heroism and skill managed to suppress the hostile fire a little and we thought he was going to get through the kill zone. I was watching his Armored Personnel Carrier. For whatever reasons he stuck his head out of that track and got hit right in the face. There wasn't much left of his head. His body slumped forward. We couldn't do anything to help. Nothing.

Gunships were on the way to try to give close-in fire support and we used up all our ammunition shooting into where we thought the enemy was hiding, but it was no good. After the captain was killed, a Sergeant took charge of that battalion and tried to move them through. Within a few minutes he too was hit and disabled. A specialist Fourth class took over and was able to direct gun fire from the helicopter gunships that finally blew a hole in the ambush and allowed the remnants of that battalion to get through.

That morning we evacuated several people that did not make it long enough to see the hospital. Their faces looked like death itself, yellow skin, dull eyes beyond help. I knew they would die and it felt so bad.

I couldn't do anything to prevent it. I think that incident shaped much of my attitude towards helping others and getting the mission accomplished. If any one event caused me to make the Medevac mission priority number one, that was it.

People have asked me, as a pilot "What made you choose to go in anywhere under any circumstance?" Simple, I didn't *ever* want to be guilty of not helping someone in need again.

Medevac

One of the most useful applications of the helicopter, the signature mission of the Vietnam war, and still one of the most important missions of helicopters today, was Aero-Medical Evacuation, "Medevac," picking up wounded soldiers from the battlefield by helicopter and getting them quickly to a hospital. The concept was first implemented in the Korean War just as it is depicted on the popular television show "M*A*S*H," with the old Bell H13's. Wounded soldiers were strapped to litters which attached to the side of the helicopters. The soldiers quickly shortened Aero-Medical Evacuation to "Medevac," and later dubbed it "Dustoff." No doubt a reference to the dusting they got as the rotor wash blew dust and dirt all over the landing zone.

In Vietnam the concept was polished into the Medevac efficiency we are all familiar with today. Each pilot knew in their heart that Medevac was *always* priority one. We performed Medevacs with Command & Control birds, resupply ships, Cobra gun ships and even the Night Hawks. There were hospital helicopters dedicated to that task, but many times we would be on site while the Medevac bird was on the ground in Cu Chi a good thirty minutes away. So when the call went out for a Dustoff, whoever was closest would pick up the wounded. Many times we would monitor the call for Medevac support and be able to get the guys picked up and to the hospital before the regular Medevac pilots would be able to even get off their helipad. Sometimes the passengers who were only trying to go from one place to another objected to being told, "We're going in on a Medevac." More often than not though, passengers relished the excitement, and several passengers got to try their hand at comforting wounded soldiers as we detoured to a hospital Medevac pad.

Picking up your first screaming Medivac is something I am sure every pilot remembers. In the midst of getting the aircraft down safely while you are under fire, checking gages to be sure nothing serious is wrong, you somehow think you are doing OK even though you are plenty busy, as you settle for a moment to see what's next, you may see two or three GI's dragging a wounded buddy. Clothes are soaked with mud and blood, his face is distorted with pain, anguish and all the emotions you can not fathom, and you begin to hear his screaming over the noise of the engine. Sometimes you would see bone protruding through a torn uniform. There was no way to understand the agony they were experiencing. The rotor wash blows blood all around and it stains the floor of the cargo area. It was not so much disgusting as it was painful in some odd way. We each dealt with that experience in our own way. For me it steeled my belief that the Medevac missions were the most important thing we could do.

Some days we evacuated 25 or 30 guys from one battle area, one time we pulled out 21 guys from a single patrol site, some of whom had been injured by friendly fire. That was sad.

One night I ran across a pilot who had fired rockets into a friendly position by mistake. He was at the very edge of dispair. No matter how much good he had done up to that point, and no matter who was at fault for giving him bad directions, he took it very hard. He will forever live with the knowledge he shot up our own men.

Sometimes we evacuated young men who had done something really stupid, like a young man who picked up a shiny new Russian pistol he saw lying in the road. He had been warned, but he wanted a souvenier! It was attached to a hand grenade and when we got to him he was missing all of his face from the nose down. We got him to the hospital in time and I am sure his life was saved, but he must have endured years of plastic surgery.

Finding Folks

Landing at a field location was always interesting. In Flight School we were taught to get the coordinates, plan the flight, coordinate with various flight following facilities en route, identify the landing site, determine wind conditions, set up an approach similar to landing at any airport, and land to a high hover.

The general procedure in Vietnam was to receive coordinates from Operations, or as happened more often than not, from some guy on the ground who was under fire. We would pick up the cargo they needed and plan the flight en route. There was very little flight following en route. When we got to the general location we contacted the guys on the ground and asked them to "pop smoke." That meant that they were to ignite a smoke grenade which we could see from the air to help pinpoint the landing site. The direction of travel and speed of smoke gave you an indication of the wind conditions. The Vietnamese realized the helicopter was most vulnerable as it hovered close to the ground. We always tried to get in and out quickly. The Vietnamese figured out early on that we were going to ask for smoke. By the time I got to Vietnam, we had to be careful.

Smoke dissipates under jungle foliage. By the time it

filtered its way up through the trees, it was difficult to identify and the color became a gray haze. Worse yet, the Vietnamese would sometimes "pop smoke" too, and you would have several patches of haze to try and identify. While that might not sound too difficult, as soon as they could, they began shooting at us. Then we had to try to dodge bullets while trying to find where the right smoke was coming from. (Just as a side note, you don't really "dodge bullets" with a helicopter, you get lucky and the bad guys miss you. We always said that because it gave the impression you controlled your destiny and the aircraft a lot more than you actually could.)

I remember the first time I tried to land at a remote fire base near the Elephant's Ear. We had received general coordinates with the caveat that the guys were on the move in triple canopy jungle. That meant that the coordinates might be invalid. It also meant they would be very hard to see from the air. Once we got to the general vicinity, I contacted the ground. They confirmed that they had moved north from their last position and had been engaged by sporadic enemy fire. To us, that meant they would be wary of disclosing their position. It is very difficult to see through three layers of jungle from 1800 feet, and we knew we would need some help identifying their location. The guys would generally make a clearing for us, but not when they were on the move. I asked if there was a cleared area in which to land.

"Roger that Little Bear! We will bring you in to a cleared area about half a click (kilometer) to our west. What is your location?"

I was disconcerted. They couldn't hear our rotor blades?

I was about two minutes out. A minute later when I called for further instructions they were under fire and too busy to pay much attention to us. Under other circumstances I might have said, "Look, I can see you guys are

busy and I don't have any particular need to get shot today. So, why don't we come back later?" But we were bringing ammunition which they seemed to be using at a rapid
rate, so we made one slow orbit to the right and called
again with a request they "pop smoke."

"Roger Little Bear. Popping white smoke now. Be advised we're having some difficulty maintaining suppressing fire on the LZ (Landing Zone)."

The gunner identified white smoke to our left, the crew
chief identified white smoke to our right, and the pilot and
I saw grayish smoke coming through two places in the
trees ahead. Oh boy! Now what? We notified the ground
that we had white smoke coming from multiple sites.

"OK Little Bear. Stand by. We will pop smoke again.
Be advised we do not have you in sight." (That is a very
discouraging message for a pilot approaching a hostile
landing zone.)

Finally their scout got us in sight and put out more
smoke. So did the enemy. Fortunately there was only one
patch of red smoke. We called to say we identified red,
purple, and white smoke. The ground troops said theirs
was red, and we began an approach into the "cleared area."

It looked all right from 1000 feet up, but as we got
closer we saw trees and lots of stumps still standing in the
middle of our intended landing site. The closer we got, the
less inviting it looked. There were fallen trees lying helter-
skelter around a clearing which was not much wider than
the disk of the main rotors. We had what helicopter pilots
refer to as "an approach to a confined area." We would
have to come to a 100 foot hover then descend vertically
between the trees.

On the way down the enemy peppered us with a few
rounds to raise our "pucker factor," but we didn't take any
serious hits. We dropped off the supplies and got out as

quickly as we could. To me the message was pretty clear. Wait till you see the smoke, and then identify the color before you start a descent. If we said "Pop red smoke" we were often greeted with red smoke from six or eight separate locations. It was less dangerous to have the ground unit tell you, "OK, Little Bear we popped smoke, can you identify?"

Combat Assaults

Formation flying was taught in Flight School, and we learned to fly safely with good separation between aircraft. In Vietnam I had to learn to fly very close to the aircraft in front of me. The rationale was that we had to put as many troops on the ground as quickly as possible, and therefore had to have all the aircraft close together. That tactical use of the helicopter was called a combat assault.

The first multi-ship lift I went on had twenty aircraft and the Aircraft Commander told me to overlap the tail rotor of the aircraft in front of me. He meant that the disc of our main rotors was to overlap the tail rotor of the aircraft in front of us. And he was serious! Flying close enough to see the other crew members was good enough for me. Being close enough to count their pimples was too much. Fortunately, most of our troop lifts or combat assaults had 10-12 aircraft, and the aircraft commander did not require overlaping rotors.

Later in my tour I flew lead aircraft on one of those huge troop lifts. That's where the flying really gets tough. As the lead aircraft, I had to plan turns, landings, and departures so that each of those aircraft in the formation could fly without over-reacting on the controls. Any sudden movement by the lead aircraft caused an exaggerated reaction in each aircraft behind it, and with the overlapping rotor blades in close formation, it could spell disaster. I never forgot the experience.

Anyone who has followed me in a group of cars on the highway is aware of how I plan turns, and even lane changes so the last car in the caravan can maneuver smoothly and safely.

The only thing more exciting than those close formation flights was the one time I flew close formation in a multi ship lift at night. Night distorts your depth perception, your ability to identify objects such as the ground, and your ability to distinguish colors. The Flight Leader allowed us to keep our position lights on, and we had a little more room between aircraft, but when I got back to the Bear Pit that night, I was exhausted with nervous tension. I kissed the ground. It was a nightmare!

A Good Night's Sleep

A good night's sleep in Vietnam had an entirely different meaning than when I was growing up in Tucson. It meant, most importantly, that you woke up, secondarily that you were somewhat refreshed, able to keep going for another day, you had not been hit by artillery or mortar fragments, and you hadn't been called out of the rack to take some outrageous mission in the middle of the night. Depending on the shift you were flying, you might get back to your hooch at 1700, have a chance to take a shower, read your mail, get something to eat and write a letter. Most of us fell asleep in utter exhaustion by about 21:00.

I have no idea how many times our sleep was interrupted as we received incoming fire during the night. Some part of the subconscious learns to discern danger and then screams a warning at you. I remember hitting the floor and then waking up to hear shell fragments zinging around me. You would be sound asleep and some sort of automatic warning system would let you know that a whining noise meant there was a shell inbound and that you had better get up and get out of the way.

Normally a round or two would come in around 23:30 or midnight, and a couple more would come in at 03:00 just to make sure you didn't get too much uninterrupted sleep. As soon as we determined we were under attack we ran for a bunker, scrambled inside, and sat quietly waiting for an "all clear." Then we would go back to bed, fall asleep, and wake up again for the "Oh-Dark-Hundred" drill. When daylight finally filtered into my room, I often found new holes in the walls or the ceiling.

There were some nights where I got scrambled out onto a mission. I would fall asleep at 21:30 and then somebody would shake me awake at 03:00 to go fly over to the Angel's Wing for extractions or insertions.

There were a few nights where Charlie and operations both allowed you to sleep all the way through the night without any incoming rounds and no interruptions. You would gently wake up to the sound of a hundred helicopters taking flight, and oh what a sense of refreshment! That was a good night's sleep.

Navigation

We all learned the same navigation techniques in Flight School. The instructors gave us some maps and some radio beacon frequencies. We planned our route, figured out how long it would take to get to certain points on the map, then "kicked the tires, lit the fires, and got airborne." We all did it by the book the first couple of times. Once we got the hang of it, we started thinking for ourselves.

There was a huge lake near the primary helicopter training center in Texas, Possum Kingdom Lake, which was a restricted area. Our TH-55 trainers had only one engine, and we flew too low to autorotate safely to shore, so the lake was "off limits." All our flights were around the lake to a variety of check points, and then back to Ft. Wolters.

That was fine in the daylight, but at night some strange
things happened. We would decide it would be nice to get
back early and go have a beer somewhere. One way to get
back early was to cut across the lake. At night the instructors couldn't see us. So some of the guys tried that. However, most of the instructors had been through the same
training, so they checked the times of arrival at all these
distant checkpoints. The little training helicopters could go
about 60 knots per hour, so when instructors divided the
distance flown by the time we were gone and found apparent speeds near 150 knots, they got wary. They watched
all our beacon lights as we buzzed around the area. Well,
we were no dummies. We turned off the lights! Strictly
illegal mind you, but a way to bend the rules.

One fateful night, my seat mate and I decided to "run
the gauntlet" with *our* lights out. We set up our alibi, found
the checkpoints we would fly to, organized flight plans,
headings, azimuths, and an extra thermos of coffee. When
we hit the sky we followed the dizzying array of lights
from fifteen other aircraft until we could safely shut off
our lights with no fear of anyone noticing. Then we took
a left turn across Possum Lake. Boy! We were gloating to
ourselves and grinning! As we looked down at the lake
that night, we couldn't see anything: no lights, no reflec-
tions, just black. We cruised along like that for about fifteen minutes. Then out of nowhere there were aircraft lights
just outside the right door! Woo Hoo Hoo! We banked
sharply to the left and turned on our lights as fast as we
could: position lights, landing light, beacons, and everything else that could even glow. While the two of us were
trying to sort out what had happened we heard an emergency radio call:

"All aircraft be advised, there is a Boeing 707 flying
low level across Possum Kingdom Lake without any lights!"
As it turned out, the guys making that broadcast were the

ones that had come up beside us. They were sneaking across the lake too, had gotten nervous and turned on their lights just before we saw them. When we turned on *our* lights, their nervousness combined with how close we were and our steep bank to the left, caused a slight distortion of perception. They thought *we* were a 707. What I learned from all that was to always keep my lights on at night.

Then in Vietnam I was told to be judicious about flying with lights on. All our aircraft had a grenade ring tied to the main circuit breaker for the exterior lights. It was just above the Aircraft Commander's shoulder where he could find it in a hurry, and in one quick motion shut off all the lights except the instrument panel.

Most of the time, both in Flight School and Vietnam, navigation was performed by dead reckoning. The essence of dead reckoning is that you check the time you have been flying, your airspeed, and heading in order to "reckon" where you are. It sounds unsophisticated, but it really did work well most of the time.

The one noteworthy supplement to navigation we made in Vietnam was the addition of references to the shape of features on the map. The four most noteworthy in the area I flew were: the Parrot's Beak, the Angel's Wing, the Dog's Head or Elephant's Ear, and Nui Ba Den which had the distinct advantage of being a real terrain feature—a 3000 foot mountain in an otherwise flat landscape of rice paddies and jungle. The other three were map features with almost no identifiable surface features. Just because some idiot draws a line on a piece of paper is no guarantee that you will see something on the ground. To make matters worse, all three of those map features were along the Air Defense Identification Zone or ADIZ for Cambodia. The ADIZ is an invisible line drawn in the sky by radar. You don't *see* a thing!

In Vietnam, pilots were assumed to know exactly where they were at all times. I don't know how many times guys

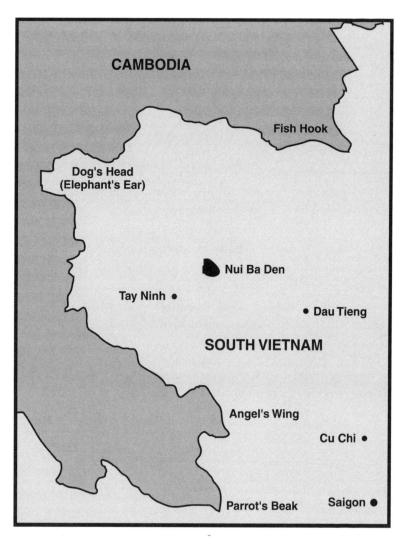

Area of Operations

on the ground asked us for a position check. Part of it I'm convinced, was a desire to hear a friendly voice. Most of the time we did know where we were and we could get "radio fixes" which allowed us to be even more precise.

A "radio fix" means we would tune in two or three different ground stations and read the radio magnetic heading indicator, which is an electronic compass. That would give us a precise azimuth or direction to the ground station. Then we would draw lines on our map in exactly the reverse direction, and where the lines crossed would be our location. However, as I said, "Most of the time."

We were not always right. One night we were doing a standard resupply with mail for a number of outposts. At about 2030 hrs. we were to deliver mail and some supplies to a particular outpost west of Dau Tieng. We established radio contact with the ground and told them we were inbound to deliver their mail. I remember telling the radio man to put out his strobe which is a very bright flashing light like you see on commercial aircraft. We knew that the guys on the ground didn't particularly like to put the strobes out in the open because, if *we* could see it from five miles away, so could the Viet Cong. And they didn't deliver letters from Mom once they found out where you were.

As a result of that hard-learned lesson, the troops on the ground took to hiding the strobe light inside various things to direct the light straight up and ensure that it could not be seen from the ground. Generally they used a "steel pot" (a helmet). But we did find one guy who hid it in a 55 gallon drum. You had to be in a turn almost precisely over him to see that one. So, anyway, we were getting frustrated when we couldn't see this guy's strobe light. I told him to go check and make sure it was on. He did. We still couldn't see the blasted things! I asked him if it was inside a 55 gallon drum. He said "no." Finally I asked him to give me his grid coordinates which is something you shouldn't do in case the bad guys were listening. He did. I began berating this poor guy on the ground, first for not knowing how to read a map, then for being lost, and I generally became obnoxious. Finally I checked the map sheet and realized I was using the wrong map. I was off by ten kilometers. I finally told him I was the one who was wrong, that I had mixed up all the map sheets in the dark, that we were ten kilometers away, and that I would like to apologize. When we finally got there at 2200, he had a cup of coffee for us—and a big old grin! God Bless that guy. He never said one bad word about the whole thing.

On other occasions, navigation errors were very costly. In June or July 1969, I was flying right seat for someone when we went to assist in a fire-fight near the Bo Loi Woods at about 10:00 in the morning. We showed up to extract wounded, but the situation became desperate with intense gunfire from both sides. We got on the ground unit's "push," or radio frequency, to see what assistance we could offer and were told the casualties were minor wounds only, to wait until the fire-fight subsided a bit.

"Little Bear it is not safe to land! Hold to the East for a few mikes."

The Cobra gunships from B company were inbound to provide aerial rocket artillery support. After a few minutes on station, we could identify a clump of trees and some heavy undergrowth where the Viet Cong seemed to be entrenched. Our people were Southeast of that patch of trees in another hedgerow with trees in it. About 150 yards of open area separated the two elements. It was fairly dry that day with artillery and gunfire kicking up lots of dust. As you orbit around a situation like that on the ground, North, South, East, and West sometimes get mixed up. You must pay close attention when you talk to them about approach paths and gun-target lines so that as soon as the word is given you are ready to go in.

The Cobras from the Diamond Heads arrived within

a couple of minutes. The unit commander described the situation to the lead Diamond Head who we all knew was one of the best Cobra pilots. They decided there was no need to pop smoke and mark locations of the friendly forces, which would make them even more obvious to the enemy. The unit commander asked them to come in on a South to North gun target line and break to the West. He described the location of the friendly and hostile forces and told the Diamond Heads to go ahead and roll in.

It never dawned on any of us that a mistake had just been made until the second and third Cobras had fired a volley of rockets.

The ground unit commander came on the radio screaming at the top of his lungs, "No! GODDAMN IT, NO! Cease Fire, Diamond Head! OH SHIT! You're killing my men! You are killing us!"

No one wants to hear that sort of call. All of us were shocked for a moment as we tried to figure out what had happened.

The pilots had fired on the hedgerow where our troops were hunkered down. Watching as our Diamond Heads shot up one of our own positions. The lead Diamond Head was mortified.

There was nothing we could do to call those rockets back. The correction was made, they shifted their fire 150 meters North and the enemy backed off, but we had casualties to pick up and these were seriously wounded.

The Cobras had fired 40 fleshette rounds. Each one had hundreds of tiny steel arrows about two inches long. Each soldier we evacuated had several fleshette wounds in him, they were bleeding profusely and those that were conscious were screaming because they knew it had been friendly fire, a mistake, and someone was to blame. Several of them had not been wearing their helmets and had fleshette wounds to the head. We picked up one load of

Nui Ba Den

eight, dropped them off at 25th Evac hospital, went back for a second load, and got six more. Other aircraft had arrived on the scene to pick up the others. A total of 26 men were hit by friendly fire that day. We all felt terrible.

I saw the lead Diamond Head pilot that night. He was inconsolable. The whole incident taught me that there are some things you just *have* to check. The location of the forces *must* be known before you fire.

The guilty party was the ground unit commander who got in a big hurry to have aerial rocket fire. I don't know if anything was ever said to him. He knew.

Recovery

Sometimes we got missions that no one wanted. One of those was to pick up KIAs. It was a very sobering mission for young pilots who thought they were invincible. Some of those missions were memorable because of the number of casualties we were recovering, other times it was the face of someone you had seen alive and well a few hours earlier, and once in a while it was because of an incident along the way.

Some of the recovery missions were to pick up people who had been dead for a couple of days in that tropical heat. The stench was enough to make you retch.

One of those recovery missions was from an open area near patrol base Diamond I or II right next to the Angel's Wing. Harassing and Interdictory fire from snipers and Viet Cong patrols had delayed recovery operations for a couple of days. It had been hot out. We knew it was going to be bad.

A ground team had gone in ahead of us to prepare the area, gather the bodies closer together and start bagging and tagging. They popped yellow smoke which also showed which way the wind was blowing and we made a normal approach to an open field. An easy landing for a change, but we had heavy hearts. The crew chief and gunner got out to help put the bodies in bags, then bring them back to the aircraft. I was flying right seat and was keeping the aircraft running so we could make a hasty departure if needed. I watched as our crew helped zip body bags shut. With the blades turning, the rotor wash kept the smell away. But when the crew brought the body bags up to the side of the aircraft the odor of death hit me. Even with the body bags zipped shut there was odor that had smeared the outside of the body bag. As the crew carefully

Resupplying the troops

lifted each of the eight body bags into the cargo area behind me, no one spoke. There were two other aircraft in
the field with us, we had our load and the aircraft commander told me to "Head for 25th Evac."

I made the departure, turned towards Cu Chi and
climbed to altitude. At about 1000 feet, the air was sweet,
and fresh. I was looking left across the cockpit when all of
a sudden one of the body bags *moved*. A hand and arm
popped out through the zipper, it made a gross moaning
noise loud enough to hear over the aircraft sounds. Maah!
The stench was awful and the movement scared the pee
out of me! Both of my hands jerked the controls. Out of
the corner of my eye I saw a black man reaching out of
that body bag to hit my face. His hand had almost touched
my shoulder!

After a few moments of adjustment we realized what
had happened. The lower air pressure at altitude caused
gasses trapped in the body to expand forcing them to es-
cape through the path of least resistance—the man's throat!
You haven't lived until you experience something like that.
When everyone figured out what happened and why the
aircraft had lurched suddenly, we started chattering and
eventually laughing. I was the brunt of a few jokes until
we got to the 25th Evacuation Hospital.

We called inbound with our cargo of recovered bodies, and were met at the helipad by some medics. They
had a little gurney or trolley they used to take body bags
into the hospital directly to the morgue. These guys were
not as careful as our crew members had been, they threw
the bodies onto the trolley like sacks of potatoes. They did
not show much respect for the dead. So, I got out of the
aircraft and ordered them to be careful. They did everything except laugh in my face.

"Lieutenant they don't care anymore. They have no

more earthly cares. This is our job. We don't try to tell you how to fly, don't you tell us how to off load body bags!"

I didn't win the argument but felt better for trying. I couldn't explain my frustration and misgivings properly. I got back in the aircraft and we left.

Vietnam Could Be Beautiful

Sometimes the night was beautiful in its own strange way. You could look out across the jungle from 1800 feet and see hundreds of parachute flares with their orange colored lights, the lights of the base camps, and on many occasions you could see position lights of perhaps forty aircraft at one time. Occasionally, there were the awe in-spiring "rivers" of red tracers from miniguns pouring out the side of aircraft.

Flying back from Tay Ninh one evening at around mid-night we decided to climb to 7000 feet and get in some "celestial navigation" time, or in other words, enjoy the ride. We climbed above the cloud layer and leveled off under a full moon with great silvery puffs of clouds rising all around us. It was one of the most beautiful sights I have ever seen.

Early morning could be beautiful also with the lush green of the jungle and that gigantic red sun so typical of the tropics. We didn't often get the chance to enjoy a cup of coffee staring at the sunrise, but once or twice I did. It was memorable.

I also remember the many mornings I would get out of the mess hall just after sunrise to see what seemed like a hundred helicopters taking to the sky. There is a distinctive roar when a large number of helicopters are in formation flight. It is followed by the semi-silence of their absence as the thunder of their rotor blades fades into the distance.

A couple of times we flew up to Cam Ran Bay, or Na Trang which were in more mountainous areas. The rolling green hills of the countryside were beautiful by any standard, and the beaches which skirted the jungle were as pretty as those in Hawaii. We saw several of those hidden coves of pure white sandy beach surrounded by hills. They were as beautiful as any the world has to offer, although you could get shot there easier than on the beaches in Hawaii. There were also hundreds of small round lagoons of blue green water all across the countryside. They were actually bomb craters which had filled with rain water, but they were very pretty—like little round swimming pools dotting the countryside.

Most of my tour was spent flying around the Mekong Delta region which was wet and very flat, only suitable for rubber tree plantations, rice paddies, and pineapple plantations. River deltas have hundreds of tributaries. I believe there were a thousand branches to the Mekong. Each of them had quaint little huts on stilts along the river banks. It was very green, and at sunrise and sunset the sunlight would reflect off of the tributaries creating beautiful silver, gold, or red ribbons. Sometimes in the early morning we would get one of those 'Science fiction" sun rises where the sun was just a giant red discoloration with various cloud shapes around and across it. Yes indeed, Vietnam could be beautiful.

Getting Shot At

I was only twelve the first time I was shot at! I was a kid in Spain. It was only a .22, but I never forgot it. The next time that I know of, was as a Private in the Army on a training exercise at Ft. Bliss, Texas. Both incidents left an unpleasant impression on even my feeble brain. So when the Army "offered me the opportunity to get shot at repeatedly on the ground in Vietnam," I opted for flight school. I thought I'd stand a much better chance of surviving while moving swiftly through the air than mired in the mud fighting Komodo dragons, mosquitoes, leaches, and other inhabitants of the jungle floor—let alone the Viet Cong.

Little did I know that I would be flying helicopters which, in addition to being much larger targets, spend a lot of time on or near the ground flying very slow. I was shot at a lot. Fortunately most of the time they missed. The sound you hear when you are shot at is the crack or sonic boom of the projectile as it whizzes past you. It is a sound you learn to detect even when you are on the radio. Often we would not hear the crack unless it was ccompanied by a slight feeling on the controls where the actual strike of the round hit the ship and you felt that hit through the control surfaces. That was especially true when you were hit in the cockpit area or in the controls themselves.

A round coming through the cockpit or the radios was very noticeable. If it came through the windshield or the side windows or doors it was a barely perceptible "crack" sound. Several times my first warning that we were under fire was the sensation from a hit through the controls to my hands.

When a bullet hit the transmission or the rotor system it was detectible within moments as instruments told the story of lost fluids and lost pressure, or you heard a new whistling sound "whee whee" as the hit blade went by, normally accompanied by a dramatic increase in vertical vibration. We all learned to deal with that in our own way. I forced myself to sound calm and cool, and tried to do everything by the numbers. Not that I was calm mind you, I just tried to sound that way. I don't remember actually wetting my pants, but there were times when I'm sure I came close. It is at times like that when you must force yourself to "hang in there just little longer."

The VIP Platoon

My first flight assignment was to the VIP (Very Important Person) Platoon, which was the third Platoon of A Co., 25th Aviation Battalion. We had UH-1D models specially configured with a huge console full of radios, secure voice encryption and decoder boxes, M-60 machine guns on both sides, and I thought I was hot snot. I didn't realize at the time that they put the new and weak pilots in VIP for a couple of months so they could learn the area, get their Vietnam wings, and fly some relatively safe missions. While I was there that rule changed so that the better pilots who had been there for a while and knew the area were assigned to VIP's. Besides, the VIP's were shot at too, so there wasn't any added safety in those missions.

There were five dedicated VIP ships, one for each of the three Brigadier Generals: (One Star) who commanded the three Infantry Brigades; another for the Division Commander (Two Star); the 5th was for the assitant Division Commander and served as back-up in case of mishaps.

The VIP ships were well cared for and painted to a high gloss with clean freshly painted floors and everything looked brand spanking new. The crews took great pride in their VIP ships as it was a way to keep flying for the VIP with somewhat safer missions, and reasonable hours. We did not pull many Medevac missions with VIP ships because that would get blood all over everything, and the VIP's didn't really like being near the ground in hostile territory.

I watched one of our "VIP's," a Brigadier General, get relieved, or in civilian terms, fired. We arrived on station at about 0800, and he made a lot of radio calls. He apparently didn't like what he heard, finally asked us to put him on the ground near the ground unit commander's bunker.

He got out of the aircraft and walked over to one of the Battalion areas. Dissatisfied with how the Battalion Commander was conducting the fight, he proceeded to tell everyone what to do. The Division Commander got wind of the situation and arrived on site with his own aircraft at 2000 feet. Tropic Lightning Six called on the Tactical Frequency, got frustrated, then contacted us directly on ship to ship radio.

"Little Bear, this is Tropic Lightening Six. Where the hell is your Code 6?"

"Sir, he got off the aircraft and is in the CP talking with the ground unit commander."

"Damn it! Little Bear, this is Tropic Lightning Six. You get your ass over there and tell him to get his ass back to the ship now! HAVE HIM CALL ME ASAP. OVER."

"Lightning Six, this is Little Bear 346, Roger that. Wilco!"

We could tell he was upset. (Our first clue was his language, and the second was that he was yelling at us over the radio.) I climbed out of the aircraft, went over to the bunkers, found the General and told him that Tropic Lightning Six wished to speak with him right now. He was fired right then and there for meddling in the Battalion Commander's prerogatives. We took him back to Cu Chi and never saw him again. There was a new Brigadier the next day.

Several of the VIP platoon missions were memorable. I remember parking right behind a self propelled 155 Howitzer and just about wetting my pants when they fired the thing without warning us. After the initial shock, we watched the crew prepare and fire several rounds into the mountain, "Nui Ba Den." It was interesting to actually *see* the bullets fly from the gun to the target. We could follow the rounds because the gun was pointed nearly horizontal to the ground and we were directly behind it.

Most of the VIP missions consisted of flying 15 to 20 minutes to some field site or fire base, then sitting on the heli-pad for an hour or more while the VIP took care of business. That short hop nonsense nearly got us killed one day. We had taken off and landed several times between 0600 and 1000 hrs. Each time we were airborne we checked in with the closest flight following facility, but none of them

told us of the impending "Arc Light." Those were an-
nounced every fifteen minutes over all the flight following
frequencies. We managed to miss them all. So, as we were
sitting quietly on the ground with all the radios off, sort of
enjoying the quiet country atmosphere, all of a sudden we
could see entire sections of triple canopy jungle being
thrown hundreds of feet in the air, and tons of dirt being
lifted up into the sky. At that point we had not yet heard
the sound that went with the scenery. But within a couple
of seconds, that hit too. It was caused by a B-52 strike called
an "Arc Light" for some reason. Coming in at 33,000 feet,
you couldn't hear the bombers. Then they released hundreds of 1000 pound bombs. It really made a mess! I understand the Astronauts could see the resulting craters from
Earth orbit. Anyway, we didn't need a cup of coffee to wake
us up that day.

Our principle mission in the third platoon was to fly
the Brigade Commanders to the sites where their troops
were based. So I did get to see a lot of the 25th Division's
areas. For awhile, in early 1969, we were flying late hours
out of Tay Ninh so many times each week that the Brigade
Commander finally found us quarters there. A couple of
noteworthy things about that assignment: First, the location of our hooch: We were close to our aircraft, close to a
mess hall, next to the on-base steam bath, and about 100
feet from a 175 inch gun. The first night we heard that
thing I was sure our hooch had taken a direct hit. It was
the next step up from "noisy as hell." When it was firing
we didn't get sound sleep. It shook everything we had.

The second thing I recall about our hooch in Tay Ninh
was the bunker we were to use in the event of incoming fire.
Most nights in Tay Ninh we did receive harassing fire. Normally it would be two or three rounds, then they would stop.

The entrance to our bunker was inside the hooch, so
we only had to get out of bed, scurry across the room and

climb in. But it was disgusting inside. The floor of the bunker was always covered with water, and the walls were wet and moldy. There were bugs, and it smelled bad. I guess it was safe. It was only about three and a half feet high, so we couldn't stand, and it must have been less than nine square feet in area. When all four of us got in there, we were elbows and knees to noses. Conditions for the soldiers in the field were a whole lot worse, so none of us complained. However, sometimes we were just too tired to bother running for the bunker and stayed in bed.

One night it didn't stop with just two or three rounds. There must have been twenty over a three hour period. We kept getting up, running to the bunker, getting wet, then drying off again so we could go back to bed. About 0100 in the morning, I heard two rounds come in and hit, each closer than the last and decided it was time to get to the bunker. I dragged myself out of bed, headed for the bunker, remembered how nasty it was in there and stopped to get my "flip-flops." *Bang!* Something very big hit the other end of our hooch. The force of the explosion blew me the rest of the way into the bunker. The next morning, as daylight began to break, we noticed we had a holy hooch! You could see daylight though hundreds of holes in our hooch. We walked around to the other end of the hooch to find a huge crater a few feet from the end of the building. It had been a 122 millimeter round!. After that, the Aircraft Commander began sand bagging his bunk. He spent several days filling sand bags and stacking them all around his bed, found some perforated steel planking to put over the bunk *and sand bagged that!* Pretty soon he had a steel reinforced bunker with a bed in it.

Once in a while the VIP missions were interesting. We were allowed to perform medevacs sometimes if they weren't too messy or if the extraction area was calm and not under fire. We were able to watch a lot of actions because the brigade commanders always went where the action was.

An artillery battalion at a Fire Support Base north of Cu Chi near a section of the river referred to as the "mushroom," fired a TOT (Time on Target) in the middle of the night. The TOT fired every gun they had at point blank range into the area just outside their perimeter. Machine guns, grenade launchers, individual weapons, artillery pieces and even some claymore mines all went off at the battalion commander's command to, "Fire"! The battalion commander and one company commander had gotten a weird feeling that something was wrong at about 1 o'clock in the morning. It was one of those dark moonless nights where the tropical humidity absorbed any starlight in the sky. They couldn't see enemy movement but had a feeling there was movement just outside the wire. They lowered all the gun tubes and pointed everything at an imaginary point 50 yards outside their bunker line. They fired all weapons point blank for a full minute.

After the TOT (Time on Target), all was quiet for a while. Then they could hear sounds and it was clear something was out there in the dark. By 0430 it was getting lighter and they could see movement. Sporadic rifle fire kept the movement to a minimum, and there was no returned fire, but it was obvious something was going on. The battalion alerted brigade headquarters that they had movement to the front in a wide arc around their perimeter. At about 0500 it was dawning enough to see there was a lot of movement, and they began to engage targets out to a range of nearly 150 meters.

I was flying a VIP ship with the second brigade commander. We got there at 0600 to see a field of extreme carnage. The TOT had killed hundreds of North Vietnamese Regular Army and Viet Cong soldiers.

While the brigade commander was in getting a briefing, I walked out to the field where the dead and dying NVA soldiers were lying. There were trails of blood off into the jungle where they had dragged away their wounded in the middle of the night. (That was so that we would not be able to get an accurate body count.) I saw a bewildering array of body parts and gore everywhere. Heads, arms, hands, legs, innards, bits of flesh. It was a grizzly sight that defies description. But, the real shocker was yet to come.

U.S. Medics were out in the field too, trying to find NVA soldiers that were still alive so they could be interrogated by military intelligence. They found a few POW's. One of them was barely alive. He looked like he was maybe 14 years old, had been hit in the chest with something large, one leg was hit with two or three 50 caliber rounds and was attached by just a few shreds of tendon. The other leg was under him at an odd angle, one arm had also been hit by a .50 and he was staring at us with the kind of look that sends a shiver down your spine. His face and skin were waxy looking. He couldn't have had much blood left in him, it was all over the ground and it was clear he was not going to live more than a few minutes.

While I was standing there with my American flight suit, my jungle hat with wings embroidered on it, fresh shaven, well fed, and clean I saw the infantry troops bringing another POW over towards me on a stretcher. He was dirty and smelled bad, had been hit in the left cheek with a M-79 grenade or a large artillery fragment. Most of his jaw and the lower portion of his face had been blown off leaving only fragments of his lips on the right side of his face. He was bleeding profusely from several torso wounds. One leg was blown off at the knee, and his left arm was obviously broken, dangling off the stretcher at a 90 degree angle. Then I saw his eyes. His eyes burned with the kind of hate you could feel. That look has haunted me for years. He had not uttered a single sound during the three hours he had been lying out there. In that bloody mass of what was left of his face, I could see his tongue, and he was trying his best to spit at me. Those soldiers were hard core and tough in a way I could never be. No matter how horribly they were wounded, none of them had made a sound that would give away their presence that night.

These Vietnamese soldiers were a whole lot tougher and more dedicated than we imagined. What was it that made these Vietnamese soldiers so motivated and tough? And, how could anyone remain silent under those conditions?

Most of our days were spent taking our VIP to some little fire base in the boondocks and waiting on the helipad for him to finish business. Sometimes we would sit there for two or three hours at a time.

One of the instruments in the cockpit is an outside temperature gauge. I remember a number of times looking up to read a temperature of 97 degrees Fahrenheit. Yes it did get hot in Vietnam, but the real problem was that constant, oppressive humidity. You just couldn't get away from it. Part of the attraction of night missions was the ability to fly with all the doors open and get some fresh night air. Those were the only times all year I remember being cool and comfortable.

Before I left the third platoon, we received new "H" model Huey's with a significantly stronger 1700 horsepower Lycoming Jet engine. The aircraft were kept immaculately clean and well polished. We wrote to car wax companies in the States and got free samples of various waxes to try on the outside of the aircraft. Those were some very pretty aircraft. One of them which we tested before and after a wax job got an extra 5 knots forward airspeed, with the doors closed of course, a fact we attributed to carnuba wax.

Taking Off in Zero-Zero Visibility

I remember taking off in "zero-zero" visibility more than once. Zero-zero means the lowest cloud layer or level is zero feet above the ground, and the forward visibility, normally reported and measured as Runway Visual Range, (RVR) was also zero. Normally the minimum weather requirements referred to as "minimums" were a ceiling of 400 feet and RVR of 1600 feet. At "zero-zero" you could barely see your hand at arms length in front of your face. In the States we would not have flown at all, but we were all given these "tactical flight tickets" which allowed us to make the decision to go or not based on the mission. I normally checked to see if there were any breaks in the clouds above the ground or at a nearby destination, and if I thought I could make it, I went for it.

I could barely see far enough to back out of the revetment. Anyway, I managed to get the aircraft backed out and turned towards the runway across the Bear Pit. When I got to the edge of Cu Chi's only runway, I called the tower for departure instructions and was told I would be on my own because the tower couldn't see the runway, let alone any aircraft which might be approaching. So he said, "You have clearance from Cu Chi tower for a tactical instrument departure to the North, but be advised, if you get in trouble, we will be unable to assist."

So I took off into the mist and fog, unable to see anything. I made an instrument departure and climbed to about 2000 feet. Within about five minutes we broke through the cloud layers. I could see patches up ahead where the clouds seemed to dissipate and we could see the mountain Nui Ba Den poking up above the clouds. About a half hour into the flight we found that the clouds had broken up near Tay Ninh, our destination. So things seemed to be working out. I gave the controls to the Aircraft Commander and relaxed. I remember looking at my flight gloves and wondering why they were so wet. I had been so tense flying without any referents that my hands had been sweating and both gloves were soaked.

There were many days when we took off in instrument flight weather conditions, and I am sure many of us felt the fear of not being able to make a safe landing if something went wrong, but there was one redeeming quality about that kind of weather.

If we couldn't see the ground, Charlie couldn't see us either, so it was less likely that we could be shot down. Not really a very heart warming thought, but every little bit helped.

Flying on instruments was particularly nerve wracking for me because in flight school I had "busted" an instrument check ride, and had an instructor tell me he was sure I would get killed in Vietnam. (Where ever he is, Nya nya Na na naaaa!) Seriously, the words from my flight instructors echoed in my mind for years and made me that much more cautious when flying during weather conditions. There were many times when we would be caught in storms, or monsoon rains and were forced to fly on instruments.

I can still hear one instructor's voice, "Airspeed, altitude, heading, trim, engine cross check, and again." Keep the pattern going and play like each one of those instruments is out to get you. Fly paranoid.

The darkest scariest flying was under the clouds in a monsoon rain at night. We often flew along just under the clouds hoping to keep as high above the ground and hostile forces as we could. Just under the overcast there is no light from above and there was never much from below. There were no house lights, no city lights to form a horizon, just inky blackness everywhere. At the end of those flights my gloves were always wet, and even though we tried to sound calm, cool and collected on the radio and on the intercom. When you got back to your hooch, and put your gear away, the wet flight gloves were a stark reminder that reality was a little less calm and cool.

Days Off

It's not like we woke up every day saying, "Oh boy! Let's go get shot at." Some days we would have a first mission at 0530, and by 0630 we would have seen enough grisly sights to last a lifetime. There were other days when we were off without much to do. Sometimes I wandered around the compound, went to the PX or barber shop which was normally staffed by a Vietnamese barber with access to a razor (*$10,000 reward?*) I could even catch a ride in a jeep to the local towns and villages. I only did that twice. Neither time was memorable. The villages were dirty with nothing to buy, and I was in constant fear that someone lurking in the bushes would pop out and shoot me. (*$10,000 reward*)

One of those ground excursions was more useful than the others. I went with the "Mess Daddy," alias Mess Steward or chief cook for our unit. He informed me why we didn't always have fresh meat. We had no refrigerator! So, of course, I took it upon myself to get us one. (But we'll get to that later.) On the way back from Long Binh, about a one and a half hour drive, I couldn't help but notice the devastation of what had once been a lush tropical jungle. I had seen Thailand's triple canopy jungle with its dense undergrowth. In today's news we see scenes from the Brazilian rain forests which are being burned and cut down. Vietnam had equally lush tropical rain forests full of wild life. Then, during the war, we took huge tractors with chains tied between them and drove around tearing down everything. It was staggering to see how flat the landscape was after the "Rome Plows" had gone through. The result was that you could see nearly to the horizon making it difficult for the VC to hide in large numbers or ambush us. I also vaguely remember the various "checkpoints" along the way where we were greeted by MP's (U.S. Army Military Police) and South Vietnamese regulars. We were briefly checked and then allowed to proceed.

While I'm thinking about it, let me put in a plug for the MP's. Those guys do a lot of good work and they are maligned by everyone. Their secondary mission is to act as infantry troops, and in my experience, they always did a super job of it.

One day off, we flew a ship to the beach at Vung Tau where we went into one of those nightclub honky tonks that stay open all day and all night. I remember an all-girl Vietnamese band singing the popular song "Rolling on the River" by Credence Clearwater Revival. With their accent, it sounded like "lolling, lolling, lolling on the liver!" I thought I would bust a gut. That was funny. We ran across a couple of guys who were stationed there. It was a standard put down to tell them we were only at Vung Tau on "vacation."

I flew to Cam Rahn Bay on a day off to visit a friend, Jim, who worked there. Cam Rahn was one of the staging areas for people going back to the States at the end of their tour. Jim introduced me to a Lieutenant, logistician, entrepreneur whose hooch was stacked to the ceiling with piles of confiscated goods: cigarettes, booze, uniforms, Soviet weapons, cameras, watches, and stereo systems. While people were out there in the field dying, he was sitting in the relative safety of his *air conditioned* hooch, getting rich.

I learned to never accept the word of a desk jockey as final. The rules he was enforcing were not even real. He just had a scam, and was getting rich. He would tell guys

"Nope! You can not take that back to the world!" You will have to leave it here. He often gave them a lot of other b.s., but rarely if ever did anyone say to him, "Bullshit! Let me see the regulation you are trying to enforce." At that point their only interest was to get back to the states and see family and friends. They did not want to start any trouble that might delay their trip home. So this guy got away with outrageous theft.

For the most part, days off were depressing. It gave you idle time to worry about the crazy things you had done recently, your girlfriend or wife in the States, and what you were missing as life continued without you. Of the many important dates in Vietnam none had more importance than the DEROS (Date of Estimated Return from Over Seas assignment). Your DEROS date was all important. Most of the guys bought "count-down calendars" or "short timer's calendars" which consisted of a picture such as a pair of boots sticking out from under a helmet. There were various versions, but they all had the same idea and purpose. They generally started with 365 numbered blocks like a "paint by the numbers" picture which you could use to count down the days until your DEROS. Each day you would fill in another block leaving you with the number of days remaining until your departure. Guys were forever bragging about their status on one of those calendars. At the 120 day mark, many started saying they were "short," meaning they only had a short time left "in country." After you got down to 99 days left in Vietnam you called yourself a "double digit midget," or a "single digit midget" once you had only 9 days left. Normally if you only had 9 days left you were too short to stop and talk about it. And there were other events planned into those calendars. One was the PCOD or "pussy cut off date," the last day you could have sex with someone and still have time to detect and get help for any venereal disease you might have contracted before you had to face a wife or girl friend back in the States. I think it was set at about 30 days. Returning to the United States was alternatively referred to as "crossing the pond" meaning the Pacific Ocean, or as "going back to the world."

Generally speaking, there was a policy that allowed guys who had been there for 11 months to take it easy for the last 30 days, but up to the last two weeks before departure we still flew orientations, mail runs and the like. One of the reasons for that policy was clerical. About two weeks prior to departure, orders had to be issued, wives notified of arrival points, and all the administrative machinery had to start up—pay checks, etc. A number of times a soldier would be killed or medically evacuated to Japan after all the notifications had gone out. That was doubly difficult to sort out and emotionally devastating to loved ones who had been told their son or husband had made it through only to find out at the airport that he wasn't on the plane.

I never had a short-timer's calendar, preferring instead to keep busy with the platoon and our missions. I flew almost every day I was in Vietnam. Most of my days off, I scrounged around for aircraft parts or other things our platoon might have needed. As a consequence, my year flew by quickly.

Milk Runs

"Maah." Everyone who knows me well has heard me say that. The expression originated during one of those routine flights or milk runs. W.O. Ed Just and I had taken off from Cu Chi on a night resupply mission taking food and mail to troops.

Within a few minutes of reaching cruise altitude (1800 feet) we ran into a storm. The first thing you notice near a storm is the turbulence. The air gets rough. We could see occasional flashes of lightning. The few flares which normally dotted the night skies over Vietnam were intermittently obscured by clouds, so we knew there was a storm. Then without any warning, we were in the clouds flying on instruments alone. All we could see were the clouds around us changing from red to black and back to red as they reflected our rotating beacon light. Red, black, red, black.

We were both focused on the instruments hoping to fly out of the clouds sometime soon. After about five to ten minutes of that your night vision gets pretty good. All lights in the cockpit are red so they won't ruin your night vision, and even our little map reading lights had red lenses. We thought we were in pretty good shape. Then a lightning bolt flashed a few feet from the aircraft followed by a hell of a noise. It was so bright we both lost our night vision—instantly. With the crash of the thunder, the startled aircraft commander turned to me with his finger on the intercom switch and said, "Maah!"

If you've ever been startled by a particularly loud crash of thunder, you know what that does to your whole nervous system. When you jump like that on the ground nothing much happens. When you are flying an aircraft where steady hands and feet on the controls are essential, jerking could have disastrous consequences. I am thankful to this day that W.O. Just was so calm at the controls. I know he influenced my behavior in the cockpit from that day on.

I asked that young pilot what "maah" meant.

He said, "I started to say something else but my finger jerked off the intercom switch before I could finish."

So, even today, when I want to emphasize that something is particularly exciting or dramatic, I say "Maah!"

What is a Normal Load?

All aircraft operate with what is called a maximum take-off weight or "maximum load." It may sound strange, but that weight changes with the air pressure, temperature, and what is called "density altitude." On a cold day at sea level, the density of the air has a certain value. As the temperature goes up, the air becomes less dense. Also, as you go up higher, the air becomes less dense. I'm sure most people are aware that it is harder to breathe at the top of the mountain than at sea level. That's because the air at higher elevations, say at 6000 to 10,000 feet, is much thinner than at sea level.

Most of the time in Vietnam we were only a few feet above sea level, but with the temperature over 90 degrees, the air was thinned out to what it would have been at 8000 feet, and the tower gave it to us in "density altitudes" of say 8800 feet. With a density altitude that high, the maximum take off weight could be reduced by several hundred pounds.

We normally took off with a full load of fuel (1800 pounds) a crew of four: pilot, aircraft commander, crew chief, and gunner carrying two M-60 machine guns with about 1500 rounds apiece—this was known as a "normal load." That left room in seats for eight people and some floor space for quite a bit of equipment. It was not unusual to take off with twelve people in addition to the crew, especially if your takeoff was from an open area where you could get a good running start.

A normal Huey with an engine operating within normal limits would consume about 400 pounds of JP-4 fuel per hour. We counted on that. If you knew you were going to make a short flight of ten to fifteen minutes, we would routinely take off with low fuel. Coming out of Saigon back to Cu Chi was a pretty uneventful flight, so many of us took off from Saigon with less than 500 pounds of fuel on board. When you did that, you could pick up three or four extra people.

I remember one day when I decided to pick up extra passengers at H-3. The procedure was, you first dropped off

your passengers and courier pouches, then picked up anyone manifested with the tower for whatever your designated
destination. When I called "Hotel Three" (Hotel Three was
the radio call name of the heliport at Saigon) they told me a
whole bunch of guys needed a ride to Cu Chi, and had been
waiting since noon. I told them I would try to help out.

After we dropped off our three or four passengers, I hovered over to the pick-up point which was somewhat similar
to a bus stop and held up four fingers to the waiting troops.
The look on their faces said, "Aw Man! Can't you take any
more?" We sat down. The first four got on with their duffle
bags, and we pulled up to do a hover check. The heat of the
day had passed, and we had plenty of power to spare, so I
held up four fingers again. With that the troops showed some
excitement, and four more came running over on the double.
When they saw they would have to sit on the floor the smiles
faded ever so slightly, but then again, they *were* getting a ride.
We picked up to a hover again. Only 280 pounds of fuel and
plenty of power left, so I motioned for more. When we finally lifted off there were twenty-one people sitting on each
other's bags, laughing and having a good time.

It wasn't exactly a "max-performance" take off, and
I'm sure the passengers had an anxious moment as we
barely scraped over the buildings at the far end of the landing area. But then again, we *were* airborne with a cooling
breeze blowing in the faces of hot dusty troops. Saigon
shrank behind us as we headed north. Fifteen minutes later
they were safe, "home" in Cu Chi. Can you imagine calling a place like that "home?"

A Female Pilot?

Some of the milk-runs had redeeming value. One day
we were sent to Saigon to pick up American Red Cross
volunteers, called "Doughnut Dollies." I think the term

"Candy Stripers" was more precise. No matter the name, they were American females, and as I recall they were all cute. It really didn't matter. By that time, any female from the States would have looked cute. As we picked them up, the rotorwash blew their skirts up to the neckline giving us a spectacular view of their legs. I'm glad they couldn't hear all the chatter on the intercom, some of which would have been embarassing, but they could certainly tell our delight from the animated faces of all those on board. We were to take them to Tay Ninh, about thirty minutes away. The Aircraft Commander immediately struck up a conversation with one of the gals. We were all paying attention to the girls instead of the aircraft until the Aircraft Commander told me to keep my eyes on my duties. Then a plan rather hatched on its own. We wrote down on a knee board what the girl should say and gave her my helmet. The Aircraft Commander and I operated the radio, but she made the call to the Tay Ninh tower with this really sexy voice.

"Tay Ninh tower, this is Little Bear 748, ten miles south for landing instructions. Over."

There was no response at first. Then the tower operator gathered his composure enough to ask us to repeat the last transmission. "Station calling Tay Ninh, repeat last transmission. Over."

She did of course, and that time the tower operator responded enthusiastically.

"Roger 748. You are cleared for approach! Call base!!"

"Call base" means to call on the base leg of the approach when you have the runway in sight. We used the base leg to check and make sure all the guns were on safe and all passengers were safely seat belted in. When we got to the base leg we had another script for our female pasenger. By then she was aware of the effect she had on the tower operator who had not heard one American female voice on the radio in about six months. She used the sexiest voice she could muster.

"Tay Ninh tower. Little Bear 748 is on base *leg*. Guns are cold and the skids are hot. Do we have permission to land?"

You could have knocked that guy over with a feather. It was all he could do to say "Roger!"

Pilots Don't Panic, Do They?

Well, not exactly, but they do get so busy they become confused. To fully appreciate this vignette, you have to understand "auto-rotations," the process whereby we land without power. A helicopter's lift comes from its rotor blades which are powered by the engine. The various turbines in the 1500 pound thrust engine spin at speeds of up to 33,000 revolutions per minute or RPM. Reduction gears transmit power to the drive shaft slowing it to 6600 RPM, and finally, the transmission turns the rotor blades at an optimum flight speed of 330 RPM. Some times on long hauls with a light load, we would reduce the engine to 5800 RPM with a rotor blade speed of 310 RPM. Anything slower than that and you would lose altitude. At anything below 300 RPM rotor speed you were gently falling. Now, when the aircraft is in a normal flight configuration and the engine quits, or when the pilot rolls off the power and lowers the collective, the blades continue to turn while the aircraft starts dropping. It's similar to putting in the clutch pedal on a car with a standard transmission. The engine is disengaged, but the car continues to roll forward. It does not come to an abrupt halt. In Flight School we practiced auto rotations, or power off landings where we would roll off the throttle, push the collective all the way to the bottom, set up an 80 knot flight attitude by dropping the nose slightly, and selecting a landing area. Then you made your "Mayday" call. Within a few seconds you would have 80 knots forward air speed and an

1800 foot per minute rate of descent. As we became more practiced with it, we could do quite a bit of maneuvering before we had to make adjustments to ensure we landed rather than crashed.

One of the dangers was that when we pulled up on the collective in a power off landing, all that vertical velocity forced so much air through the rotor system that it could over speed the rotor blade. 330 RPM was normal, but 340 RPM would over stress the rotor system. *If the blades stayed on the aircraft*, it would have to go into maintenance for a complete overhaul—a very expensive and time consuming process. One of the things we did as part of our practice was that whoever was not flying would call out RPM, descent rate, altitude, airspeed and any other useful information to the pilot or Aircraft Commander. You were supposed to do it in a calm, professional manner for multiple reasons, principle among which was to avoid adding excitement to distract a very busy pilot from critical activities. In Flight School, if things weren't going well, you could always roll on the power, recover and try again. But we practiced a lot so that when you finally did have an engine failure, your reflexes would go into "semi-automatic" mode, and you would do everything right. (I have often thought of the crew of Apollo 13, a flight to the moon that went seriously awry. They never had time to be frightened. They executed one emergency procedure after another until something finally worked.) In my experience, people will do exactly the same in real life as what they do in practice. Every practiced forced landing in Flight School was to a corn field, and the training required the Pilot to call out "Mayday" three times and report that he was landing in a corn field. Never mind the fact that there were no corn fields in Vietnam.

One of our aircraft tail numbers was 186, and it was one of the oldest in our unit with close to 3,000 hours on it—many of us had received hits in that aircraft. It was repaired, put back in service, and we flew it some more. As with all things it started getting old and crotchety. Each day after flying, when we shut the aircraft down for the day, we performed a "post flight inspection."

One day aircraft number 186 failed an inspection at a time when mission requests were at an all-time high. It failed something major like tolerances on the main rotor system, or high torque readings during a hover check. (That would indicate the engine had ingested too much sand or a piece of metal and had sustained internal damage.) I'm not really sure what the initial failure was. When the pilots mark the log book with a failure they make a red "X" next to the column for flight status of the aircraft, meaning it should not be flown. Then they report that status to flight operations to make sure the aircraft is not scheduled for a flight until the Maintenance Officer has checked and fixed the problem, or worked off the deficiency. During war time situations, the Maintenance Officer is empowered to authorize a one time flight with certain "red X'd" conditions still present. The Maintenance Officer draws a circle around the pilot's "X," thereby authorizing the aircraft to be flown in "Circle red X'd" condition for one more day. So it happened with 186. She was "red X'd" by the pilots and "circle red X'd" by Maintenance every day for 29 days in a row. We were too busy to do anything about it at the time. But as pilots were assigned 186 they began to be cautious with her. Word slowly got around that we were pushing one of our oldest ships considerably harder than was prudent. But, we were also aware that Maintenance had its hands full with a number of ships undergoing 25 and 100 hour maintenance inspections which required a day or two to complete if all the parts were available. Maintenance was behind schedule, and they were being disrupted by mortar attacks the same as everyone else. So we continued to fly

186 in "circle red X'd" condition. Pilots would tell each other of the hover limits on 186, and the amount of torque needed to get her airborne. I flew it on day 18 or 19, again on day 25 or 26, and on day 30.

A young Warrant Officer by name of Ziolkowski was assigned as the Aircraft Commander with me on day 30. We had to take some people and equipment from Cu Chi to Tay Ninh. We pulled out of the revetment, picked up whatever we were supposed to carry and hovered over to the edge of the runway for departure instructions. "Ski" noticed that the hover took about 48 pounds of torque even when we were only a couple of feet off the ground, so we continued at a low hover and got ready for a minimum power take off. That's where we push the nose forward slightly without increasing engine torque by more than a pound or two, and very slowly gain speed until we get to 18 knots. At that point the helicopter airframe goes through "translational lift" and the airflow through the rotor system begins to provide sufficient aerodynamic lift to begin climbing. Note that I said "begin climbing." It does not do so in a big hurry. A normal power setting for departure causes a climb rate of 500 feet per minute, but then again, a normal power setting for that climb rate is about 45 pounds of torque. Old 186 was requiring that much power just to hover three feet off the ground.

We took off and were climbing at about 100 feet per minute and 40 knots (where 60 is normal and 80 preferred). To prevent the possibility of one of the jet jockeys or a C130 flying up our rear end by accident, we notified the tower that we were over gross weight and making a slow departure to the north. As I said earlier, a helicopter can make a normal power off landing if it has 50 to 80 knots airspeed and about 1000 feet altitude. You can do with a little less altitude if you have more airspeed, or do with less airspeed if you have enough altitude to start some sort of dive to gain airspeed. We practiced doing some auto rotations where we would be at 80 to 100 knots and 100 feet, and we practiced a few at 1500 feet and only 40 knots. They all worked fine in practice during Flight School. But back to the story.

Within a couple of minutes we were at 60 knots, about 600 feet of altitude, but only two or three miles off the north end of the runway. Then came this tremendous BANG! We felt all kinds of shrapnel poking holes in the tail section, and lost all power. Ski dumped the nose instinctively to try and get some airspeed, but the ground was awfully close, so he pulled back again. We had been struggling to gain altitude so he (naturally) did not want to lower the collective and loose any of that hard earned altitude. (Big Mistake.) I flipped the radio to Guard and told him we were on Guard. He made the call. Keep in mind we were dropping at about 1800 feet per minute with a full crew, five passengers and full load. We could see that impact was going to be both soon and rough.

"Mayday, Mayday, Mayday! Cu Chi tower, this is Little Bear 186 on guard. Engine failure off the north end of the runway. Going down in a cornfield....I mean a...er...a rice paddy."

Meanwhile I was watching the altitude, airspeed etc., and was alarmed to see the collective was still up bleeding our rotor RPM down to about 300, so I was busy trying to push the collective down, and Ski was pulling it up. By now we were at only 300 feet and dropping like a rock. It was exciting, and my voice said so. "Rotor RPM below 300! Airspeed 20 knots." But, like I said, "Panic?" Naah. Just awfully busy.

I heard the tower respond, so I knew we would be picked up. I had no idea what they said. We were 200 feet off the ground with dangerously low rotor RPM, barely 20 knots of forward airspeed, and needed to do something quick. Ski dumped the nose again, and we were both amazed at how fast the ground started to come up at us.

Ski pulled back on the cyclic and tried to find a landing spot. No airspeed, no altitude. *We were going to have a rough landing!* "We're going for the paddy in front of that dike!"

Just before impact we noticed barbed wire in the rice paddy and both of us tried to react. (Not a good idea.) The collective was way up again and I was trying to get it up even higher. Instead of the familiar "wop, wop, wop" of the rotor blades, we were getting a distinct "whoosh, whoosh" and the best I can determine, the rotor RPM was down to about 240. When that happens all the controls are very sluggish. So, Ski kept pulling back on the cyclic in an attempt to slow our forward airspeed which was still about 20 knots. At about 20 feet, old 186 fell out of the sky and hit the rice paddy. It was still moving forward, so we picked up the barbed wire. Ski's last efforts on the cyclic finally paid a big dividend. We had hit the ground in a level attitude (Thank God). However all that pulling had brought the cyclic back against the seat between his legs, and as

Preflight Inspection

the blades went around for the last time, they flexed down and chopped off the tail boom with a resounding "whack." The skids had been spread apart from the impact. I kind of knew we wouldn't get a broken wing award for that one. (The Broken Wing Award is an honorary award given to pilots who bring in a crippled aircraft without additional damage or injury to crew members.)

The passengers were looking rather stunned and were wondering what to do next. Ski started hollering, "Get out!! Get away!! It's gonna blow up!" You never saw anyone get out of a helicopter so fast! He had his seat belt and restraints off, chicken plate back, the door open, and was off through the mud leaving a "rooster tail" of mud and water as he ran for cover. I turned to the stunned passengers and told them to go for cover, and proceeded to perform all the shut down checklist items: cyclic locked, collective down and locked, main fuel off, radios off, lights and rotating beacon off, main power bus off, battery off. Finally I opened the door and stepped out to the ground. (Normally I had to step down to the top of the skid first and then down to the ground, but the skids had been squashed outward with the force of impact.)

Ski was still hollering at me from behind the rice paddy dike. "Geddown! It's gonna blow up!" But by then it was obvious there was no more danger of explosion. It was just a very dead helicopter which had served its purpose well. It had probably evacuated over 1000 wounded GI's, had fired thousands of rounds in fire suppression, delivered several tons of mail from home to soldiers in the field, resupplied soldiers in need with food, ammunition and supplies, and had been one of the prime experimental platforms used to try out numerous innovations. In her last flight 186 had forgiven two of us for multiple errors, and set us down safely enough that no one was hurt.

I walked over to the rest of the passengers and crew

members noting that we were in enemy territory and all I had was a .38 caliber pistol. Aaaw Man! Here we go again. *$10,000 reward!* Within thirty minutes we were picked up by another helicopter, shuttled back to Cu Chi, and given the rest of that day off. There weren't any extra helicopters available.

LITTLE BEAR "TWO-SIX"

*Management is the art of counting beans. Leadership
is the art of making every being count.*

The Company commander Major Caryl Marsh had
been watching me carefully and was evaluating my
ability to be a leader as well as my abilities as a
pilot in various types of missions.

By September of 1969 I had accumulated a lot of flight
hours, a number of statistical "attaboys" for the number of
soldiers medically evacuated, and several medals, but I also
racked up quite a few "ass-chewings" for doing "no, no's."
In short, I had a reputation for being a good pilot but a bit
of a maverick. I had been in the thick of it a number of
times and managed to get everybody home safely, but the
CO was forever calling me in to bawl me out for something
or another.

It is fair to say Major Marsh wondered about my judge-
ment and probably rightly so. I had proven I was brave, pos-
sibly even too brave, but I had gotten in hot water for con-
fronting senior officers and even for "harassing" a full bird
colonel. Major Marsh was evaluating me for a position as platoon leader, and I was getting to be a senior lieutenant. The
"Old Man" had to evaluate my ability to manage assets, time,
and missions and my ability to fly.

Other pilots I flew with provided him with feedback on my ability to fly and "fight" a helicopter. I was doing OK on that account, but not spectacular. I was not a "great" pilot.

Major Marsh was more interested in my ability to lead and influence others. My heart was always in the right place. If I could only stay out of trouble for a couple of months.

Wagging Low

On the 21st day of September, I had taken a new aircraft, 437, out on a mission. It had received two or three hits. Small arms fire: you know, a couple of minor rifle bullets. No one was hurt, and the aircraft was flying fine. However, that aircraft had been promised to the VIP platoon, and we were not in the habit of giving VIP's aircraft that had been shot up. So as I called the Bear Pit for parking instructions, the CO himself came on the radio.

"Four Three Seven, this is Little Bear Six! Set that aircraft down and get your ass in my office NOW! Out!

Here I go again. I turned the aircraft over to the pilot and walked over to the CO's office for my "ass-chewing," hoping it was something easy to explain. I was going over in my mind what I could have done different that day to avoid getting shot up. I knocked on his door and heard the First Sergeant holler "Come in." (I thought, Oh, no. Whatever it is, its bad enough he wants a witness.) If I were a dog, I would have walked in with my tail wagging low between my legs. Anyway, I slinked in the best I could, came to attention in front of his desk and saluted.

"Sir, Lieutenant Finch reporting as ordered!"

"Lieutenant!? Can't you get anything right?"

"What did I do now, sir?"

"Well first of all you got the rank wrong. I have a set of orders here that show you are promoted to Captain. Next, I hear you managed to get holes in another new aircraft.

But, I did get a call from the Wolf Hounds saying they appreciated your support, so we'll let that one go. I'm assigning you as platoon leader Second Platoon. Lastly, did you reserve a table at the club so we could all have a beer on you tonight?"

We did go to the club. And I'll never forget that promotion. What a relief. Our hooch maid was especially proud to sew on my Captain's bars. "No more *Trung We*. Now you *Di We*," she said. My heart was dancing with pride.

Combat Support Platoon Leader

Having proven my navigation skills and with a few hundred hours of Vietnam flying time to my credit, I "graduated" to the Second Platoon, Combat Support. I signed for nine aircraft, a complete airfield lighting system, several sets of tools, and some miscellaneous equipment worth a total of about $10 million. I was 24 years old.

I was now responsible for 36 lives and execution of a wide variety of daily missions in support of the 25th Infantry Division. The second platoon missions were combat insertions, extractions, medical evacuations, and a variety of other combat support missions. Combat insertions were those missions where we picked up a full load of troops and dropped them off in landing zones which might be clearings in the trees, rice paddies, open areas or bomb craters. Combat extractions were missions to pull the guys out and bring them back to a base camp somewhere. Extractions were normally "hot," meaning you *were* going to get shot at. But the real danger was in the insertions because you never knew *if* you would be shot at or not, and had no idea where the enemy was. We took a lot of hits doing both insertions and extractions. At least in the extractions someone on the ground could tell you where the Viet Cong were and you could suppress or return fire.

In 1969, the Little Bears tried a lot of innovative ideas. I was vaguely aware that our unit was trying to increase or refine the type of support we could provide. The second platoon was right in the middle of all those innovations.

At one point around May 1969, we tried using an arrangement of wooden crates on the side of the aircraft as racks for dropping 81 millimeter mortar rounds. It was hopelessly inaccurate and many of the rounds failed to go off. They would destabilize in flight and tumble. The really bad news is that we got those ones back at night fired from a Viet Cong mortar tube. They exploded as they were designed to when fired that way.

The Nighthawk was another innovation. The idea was to take back control of the fighting at night. We mounted an infra-red searchlight and a white light searchlight, borrowed from the M-60A1 tank to assist firebases in identifying, chasing and engaging the enemy.

The first version was with two M-60 machineguns mounted side by side. That was an improvement in firepower but not a substantial or marked improvement over the standard M-60. Then we tried a .50-caliber machine gun. We used a very bright Xenon light (two million candlepower search light like those things they point up into the sky for grand openings). It had an integrated Infra red capability, mounted a .50-caliber machine gun with it, on the left side of the aircraft. That .50-caliber had such a kick when it started firing that it would tear up the tail boom. After about 2-3 hours of flying while firing that .50-caliber, the post flight inspection showed the metal at the beginning of the tail boom had cracked and was starting to tear through. The tail boom was in danger of falling off. So the .50-caliber did not work out well with the UH-1D Iroquois ("Huey").

During my tour, about June or July, I flew an "H"

model Nighthawk that had a Mini-gun. This was a General Electric, electrically operated 6 barrel Gatling gun that fired about 4000 rounds per minute. It was mounted on the left side so the aircraft commander had better control of the gun. The infra red searchlight capability allowed us to acquire targets at night without the enemy knowing what we were up to, then we could switch on the Xenon light. That allowed both the Infantry on the ground and the air crew to engage the enemy.

The high-speed, 4000-rounds-per-minute mini-gun was astounding. It put out an incredible volume of fire. You could literally fill a football field with bullets in just a couple of seconds. Once the concept was refined, the gun and the searchlight were mounted together on a steel plate toward the back of the cargo area. The steel plate dissipated the energy from the recoil of the gun making a very effective weapons platform. It didn't tear up airframe too badly.

The Vietnamese figured out that that thing was devastating, so if they thought you were a Nighthawk, they wouldn't shoot at you at all. Sometimes we found ourselves getting a little crazy. We'd turn all the lights on, so we looked like a re-supply ship. we'd hover down, nice and slow, at about 200-300 feet, looking for all the world like we were trying to find a place to land, just itching for someone to shoot at us. The intent was that, once we drew fire, we'd turn that mini-gun around and devastate an area pretty quickly. Most gunners firing those things were Pathfinders. They weren't part of the Aviation unit itself, but specially trained, experienced infantry guys from within the 25th Division. They knew what to do with that mini-gun. It wasn't anything that the pilots were able to do particularly well, but those gunners were extraordinary at being able to train that firepower on a target.

There were a couple of little glitches with that system.

First, you had to learn how to fire the thing. If you just told people to fire whenever they had a target, they might wait 2, 3, 10 or even 25 seconds. When the gunner opened fire, there was a bright flash of light from the muzzle of the barrels, a whole lot of torque applied against the side of the aircraft, and more noise than anyone could stand. The shock and surprise of it all was a real jolt to the nervous system and it would ruin your night vision. If you weren't ready for it, the kick from that mini-gun would throw the aircraft way out of trim. An employment technique quickly evolved. When they identified a target, the Pathfinder would let me know first so I could steel my nerves. I reserved the right to give the order to fire, and I'd kick pedal to compensate for the torque as he opened fire. Another slight problem was the rate of fire. A UH-1 could only pick up a certain number of rounds (10,500 I think), and with that rapid rate of fire you would be out of ammunition in a matter of two minutes, so we had to control the fire very carefully and even then we had to re-arm frequently.

Another idea we tried in 1969 was the flame bath. The flame bath was three 55-gallon drums of fougasse (jellied fuel) strung together with whatever we had at the time; rope, netting, or a cargo net, mesh, whatever we had. We'd tie the three drums together, and attach a trip flare to the cargo hook under the aircraft. As you released the load, the trip flare would go off. The barrels started to separate on the way down. When it hit the ground and spread out, the flare ignited the jellied fuel. It would make a huge fire ball on the ground roughly similar to the high drag 500 pound napalm bombs dropped by the Air Force F-4s. The flame bath was hard to control, because you had a 1500-pound weight hanging at a long pendulum arm underneath the aircraft. When you made a turn, that mass would swing you out to the right or left. Pilots would try to straighten out, but there was this weight holding you back. It was a very unusual load to contend with. I remember flying with telephone poles slung beneath us in Thailand, that was about the same. It was way down below you and very difficult to control the movements of the aircraft. It would feed back to the controls quite a bit.

The other challenge about the flame bath was aiming it. There was no sighting mechanism on a UH-1 Iroquois "Huey." So we painted stripes and cross hatch marks across the chin bubble (plexiglass windows) below our feet, in between the pedals. You'd aim down that stripe across your controls, between your feet. You'd look at those lines, kind of sighting between your anklebones with these little yellow lines on your chin bubble. Some were for 60 knots and some were for 80 knots, depending on what drop speed you were able to use.

We got fairly accurate. The first time you always made mistakes. Whoever was flying as check pilot next to you always gave you all sorts of grief about what was your drop altitude, your speed, what kind of an angle, yaw, and what other control movements had you put in when you released the thing. You were really punching off a sling load and hoping you could predict where it would land. It was a one-thumb-action deal. You'd push the one button with your thumb, and it would fall off. It hopefully would catch fire and blow up on the ground.

Another problem with the flame bath that no one told us about was that, in Vietnam, there was no such thing as a cold target. It wasn't like some gunnery range back in the U.S. The enemy had a habit of shooting at you when you were trying to learn to drop that thing. The first two times I tried to drop a flame bath, I was trying to learn how to do this, and people were shooting at me in the middle of trying to drop the thing on target.

I got slapped on the helmet by Ed Behne, our warrant

officer instructor pilot, one time. He yelled at me, "What the hell were you doing with that thing?"

I couldn't remember the altitude and answer all the questions. Finally I said, "Look, I was getting shot at, and I was doing the best I could. I don't know where it hit."

The other problem we had with the flame bath was that, if you dropped it too low, the heat from the flame would bubble the paint on the bottom of the aircraft. The crew chiefs didn't like that at all. One last problem we worried about a little at the time was if you have an engine failure at a maximum performance hover with a big load, where do you try to hit the ground so that all that FUGAS didn't blow up under you?

Forced Trim

In Flight School we learned about the Trim Tab to help with instrument flights and to set the aircraft for hands-off flying for limited periods. In Vietnam it had another purpose. There were a variety of low level missions such as the "sniffer and defoliation" missions where you spent a lot of time at high speed trying to collect grass stains on the bottom of the skids. In defoliation missions, most of the time was spent at 80 knots right at the top of the trees, and you would occasionally hit a branch or a bird, etc. So, just in case whatever you hit came through the windshield and knocked you silly for awhile, we flew with our visors down, set the forced trim in a climb attitude, and forced the cyclic forward to fly the mission. If you did relax your grip on the controls, the forced trim would start you into a fairly steep climb which would give you a few moments to wipe the mess off the windshield (and off your face if necessary).

Defoliation missions were nasty. We rigged the aircraft with a 400 gallon tank of defoliant and a long boom with nozzles that stuck out the sides of the aircraft. The equipment used was similar to that you see on helicopters used for crop dusting in the States. Sometimes we flew what was called Agent Orange. Other times it was a less corrosive version of chemical agents designed to take all the leaves off trees. It worked well. We could spray a section of the trees along a road one morning, and by the next afternoon all the leaves would be gone along with all the birds, monkeys, and other wildlife. When that corrosive chemical got on the aircraft it would peel off the paint. I got some on my left leg one time and it burned for days. Even today, 30 years later, I get recurring boils and blisters on that spot. (My wife claims it is the meanness coming out of me.)

The "Sniffer" was another application of the helicopter we tried in the 25th Aviation Battalion. The aircraft was outfitted with a chemical analysis unit and hollow metal tubes which stuck out each side of the aircraft. An Army Chemical Corps officer flew with us to monitor the instruments. We were directed to fly very low at moderate airspeed over areas of suspected enemy concentration, and the chemical spectrum analyzer would detect enemy locations. If the equipment detected the presence of enemy soldiers, an orange light came on and an audio signal beeped enemy presence. We marked the location and relayed the coordinates to an artillery battery for a fire mission. We didn't fly that type of mission very often. It was very dangerous, and I'm not sure if it had a high success rate. I am aware of at least one time where it did locate enemy soldiers, confirmed by our survey of the site after an artillery barrage. It does sound strange that the enemy *smelled* different, and I'm not sure how the thing worked.

It may have detected the presence of humans, or their camp fires, or something else. As far as we were concerned, it was simply another mission which required us to fly very close to the ground reducing room for error in a war which was none too forgiving. Each of the Little Bear pilots who flew that mission came back with a different tale. Mine was rather mild. During one of the turns, I got too close to the trees and the rotor blades chopped off the top of a tree. Other than my shock at having done that, no particular damage was evident.

One of the other Little Bears hit a large bird like a hawk or a buzzard which came through the windshield and smacked him in the face. But that wasn't enough. The thing wasn't completely dead, so in addition to the shock of hitting something (which pilots don't like to do) and the sudden rush of wind in his face, the bird started flapping around in the cockpit. Feathers were everywhere, and either a claw or a beak stabbed the Aircraft Commander in the leg. The "forced trim" took them up to 1000 feet while they were otherwise occupied. When they were able to turn their attention back to the aircraft, they were safe. But they had enough fun for that day, so they came back to the Bear Pit to re-arm, re-fuel, re-window, and (it is rumored) to change their drawers. It did make believers out of the rest of us when we saw what a bird strike could do to a Huey. After that, we all used the "forced trim," and put the visors down on our helmets like good boys.

The Immelman

At about the 750 flight hours mark, pilots run into a statistical "wall." That magic hour mark is when you will likely have an incident or an accident. I think a level of overconfidence causes it. In 750 hours of helicopter flight time you make a lot of landings and take offs. In a commercial jet you fly two, three, five hours or maybe more on an international flight and make 1 landing. In a helicopter it was often a matter of minutes between landings, many of which were hard or stressful, and I suspect it was normal to have six to ten landings per flight hour. After you survive that many near misses with death you begin to think you are invincible or something. You get carried away with your own puffed up confidence. Then you have an accident or an incident.

I remember pilots returning to the Bear pit bragging about how much grass they had on their skids from low level flying at high speed. To a jet jockey, low level flying is anything lower than 500 feet above the ground. To most of us fling wing types, low level was 25 to 50 feet above the highest obstacle. But there was always someone willing to push any limit established. So, some pilots were out there below the tree line at 80 knots with the skids in the elephant grass, hopefully praying there wasn't an elephant or a water buffalo hiding in the grass ready to rear up in fear as they went by.

A corollary danger many of us discovered the hard way was that you were so focused on the ground and the immediate horizon that you sometimes missed trees off to your left or right. When you had to make a quick turn sometimes the rotor blade would hit a tree or the branches of a tree and knock the blades "off track." That would start an immediate one to one vertical bounce or vibration in the aircraft that would eventually shake the airframe apart unless corrected.

The maintenance people corrected the problem fairly easily so it was no big deal, so long as you took it easy on the aircraft and reported it soon. The Hueys required careful maintenance which included daily pre-flight and post-flight inspections, a thorough inspection every 25 hours, and a 100 hour Periodic Evaluation or PE which examined the structural metals for fatigue, and made a very detailed and thorough inspection of every assembly and component on the entire system from radios and flight controls to fuel pumps, electromechanical switches and the Geezus nut on the top of the rotor blade system. At the end of such an exhaustive maintenance effort including assembly and disassembly of major components, the Maintenance Officer and the crew chief would test fly the aircraft. He would put it through its paces, and measure power settings required for a variety of maneuvers and operations.

Maintenance officers were accomplished pilots and had a very specialized job, one for which we were all thankful that they performed well. One thing the Maintenance Officers did not do is fly combat missions, and they missed that. In spite of how critical they were to all of our safety and the incredibly complex test flight they had to perform, they felt like they weren't really combat pilots and that somehow they weren't doing enough. On my days off or "down," I still hung around the flight line or the maintenance hanger in case there was some flying to do. The Maintenance Officer, Lieutenant Bill Bailey was a bit envious of the "real pilots." He was also a friend. One day Bill asked me if I would like to go out on the test flight with him. I said, "Sure," so we suited up and went for a test flight.

I was sort of content to sit in the right seat and watch all the hover checks, torque settings, exhaust gas temperature readings and get an occasional comment from the test pilot. Then he said something like, "Why don't you take us out into the local area and show me how you real pilots fly?" (Sound like an invitation to disaster to you too? It didn't to me because I was at the magic 750 hours.)

I do not remember all the things we did, but I do remember saying, "Sure, I can show you how to do a Himmelman! Watch this!"

At about 300 feet, 80 knots, and cruise power setting, I pulled back firmly on the cyclic, raising the nose of the aircraft and we went straight up. I mean *straight* up, 90 degrees to the ground! All you could see was sky! We climbed a few hundred feet up like that until the aircraft forward airspeed reached zero. We became weightless as we began to fall back to Earth. Then I kicked right pedal firmly and we watched the nose come around until all you could see was ground, but the ground was awfully, awfully, close. We picked up a lot of airspeed very quickly, dropping like a homesick brick. I pulled back on the nose and it began to shudder. The aircraft was under a lot of stress with excessive airspeed in a very steep dive. I was pulling back on the cyclic harder and harder. I could feel the "G" forces and the strain on the airframe, but we were still in a steep dive.

At some point I realized the error of my ways. I had not made certain I had enough altitude to enter that maneuver, bled off way too much airspeed trying to show off to the maintenance officer, and I was not able to pull out of that screaming dive at now over 120 knots. The ground was rushing at us at very high speed, I was trying to level the aircraft, and eventually decided to pull up on the collective to induce a more radical attitude change. For a second or so I thought I had it made. It almost worked. Then we hit a rice paddy dike at about 100 knots, flipping the aircraft over upside down and bouncing probably 50 feet back up into the air, slamming back into the mud where we hit with a disgusting *Thwack*, and then stopped dead. I was upside down with my face in the water. The windshield had broken and pieces of plexiglass had stabbed me in the face, cut my nose and forehead. All of my weight was hanging on my seat restraints so I couldn't release the harness. Finally, I forced my head under water, straightened out as best I could, and was able to take enough weight off the harness to release the buckle. Then, I rolled over onto one shoulder and crawled out from under the steaming wreck of what had been, moments earlier, a magnificent flying machine.

The crew chief had been ejected from the aircraft upon impact and landed in the muddy water 35 feet away, he was unharmed, shaken and more than just a little peeved that after all that work in the maintenance hangar, his aircraft was a pile of scrap. The maintenance officer broke his arm, I was bruised and shaken, broke my left hand, and had multiple cuts to my nose and forehead from the windshield. We were dazed, stumbling around in the rice paddy for a while, then someone picked us up. The worst part is that I felt so stupid. No one was seriously injured, but the aircraft was a total loss, and it was all 100% avoidable. I was in trouble with the C.O. again, and rightly so this time. You know, I don't think that maintenance officer ever flew with me again. We were both in a cast for a while, so it cramped our ability to fly.

John Wayne

I remember an incident when we were trying to insert some troops in an open rice paddy near Canh Tho. We normally tried to set one skid on a dike to stabilize the aircraft and make it a little easier for the guys to get off the helicopter. But then, there were always these "John Wayne" types who climbed out onto the skids and started jumping off before you got all the way down. That caused the aircraft to rock or shift around in the wind. Well, on this particular occasion, two big guys jumped off the same side of the aircraft at the same time, and I was having a heck of a time keeping things under control.

The next thing to go wrong was that I couldn't find the stupid dike to rest my skid on. I kept searching for it and sinking in water, then pulling up a little to resettle.

We started receiving fire from our front and the right side, and everyone began yelling at me. You can't yell back because you're too busy. The lead aircraft is telling you to get going; the Aviation Unit Commander is on another radio telling you you're being shot at; the guys are hollering all kinds of things; the Commander of the ground unit is calling on a third radio telling you to hurry up because he needs the rest of his men to return fire at the enemy. The next thing I knew everyone decided to jump off at the same time and of course the aircraft popped up about six feet in the air making us a very handy target even from 250 yards away. I looked out the side window in time to see the last of the jumpers. He was a short soldier, perhaps 5'2" tall with full combat gear and a M-60 machine gun strapped on his back. He hit that water and went all the way under. The only thing you could see was his steel pot floating on the surface. Then he came up sputtering, spitting and fighting mad. Well, with all those Viet Cong shooting at me, and this American soldier ready to shoot me too, I didn't need any further coaxing. I dropped the nose, pulled pitch, and got the heck out of there.

Flame Baths

Something else I learned in the Second Platoon was how to drop "Flame Baths," As I said earlier, it was three 55 gallon steel drums filled with napalm and petroleum jelly hooked together in a cargo net with three flares to light the napalm upon impact. It was not a simple matter to drop the thing. First you had to call the Ammo Point and tell them to rig it up. Then you had to come to a steady hover over this huge explosive charge while two or three guys hooked it to the cargo release under the aircraft. The cargo hook looks like an upside-down question mark with a flap of metal that can be released/opened from inside the cockpit by a control on the Aircraft Commander's cyclic grip. Keep in mind that the AC's grip has a variety of buttons, switches, and triggers, and you have to remember which goes to what equipment. Some are for radios, others are for flight controls such as the "trim switch." In the early days of helicopter operations there was no light to tell us the cargo hook was "armed" or released. When one of the guys came out from underneath the aircraft and gave you a thumbs up, that meant he thought you were good to go. There were a couple of incidents where the guys took off thinking all was in order and dropped the load a few yards away with disastrous results. By the time I started playing with them, safety devices had been incorporated. One was a long rip cord which acted as a safety valve. If the load didn't fall at least 25 feet, the ignition flares wouldn't light and therefore would not ignite the napalm.

So you hovered over to the ammo point while a ground crew hooked up this 1500 pound load and told you to go. The aircraft strained to pick up that kind of load from a 29 foot hover, especially when you had a full load of fuel (1800 lbs.). All the controls got sluggish. Then you had to call the tower for special departure instructions so you didn't over-fly occupied buildings, etc. Departure instructions were almost never "into the wind." You departed at maximum gross weight, barely even climbing till you got up to 60 knots. Then you found something like a simple turn took a lot of extra planning because now you were about as aerodynamic as a pregnant whale with this bomb swinging like an enormous pendulum twenty-five feet below you. When you tried to turn, it tried to keep going straight! Any erratic control movements were at first delayed, then exaggerated by the load swinging below you. Once you mastered those changes in your aerodynamics, then came the "what next?" How do you drop it with any accuracy at all?

F-4 pilots learned bombing techniques in their flight training, and the F-4 came with bombing sights. Helicopters, of course, did not. They were never intended to be used as bombers—let alone rigged to drop 1500 pounders. Well, the Army was never one to be outdone by our baby brothers in blue, so we took to painting lines on the chin bubble right between the pedals. That sufficed as a sort of sighting grid with left & right limits set by our feet and the horizontal lines as a crude cross hairs. But different speeds and altitudes caused the "bomb" to travel differently: further, if you traveled faster or higher, and less horizontal distance, if you were close to the ground or in a dive. As we closed in on my first "practice target." We were hit by hostile ground fire twice before I finally released the Flame Bath and started a climb out of the target area. As soon as we were free of that 1500 pound load, the aircraft had all kinds of extra get-up-and-go, and I made a left hand turn to see what damage had been done. The instructor who had been very patient until we got hit now began to berate me with all kinds of questions:

"What was your airspeed at release, Lieutenant?"

"At what altitude did you release the load 'L-T'?"

"Which sighting line did you use?"

"How far did you miss the target by?"

About the only coherent response I gave was, "Hey, dirt bag! You told me this was a practice target. No one said it was going to be shooting at me!"

But then, we both knew that all targets in Vietnam were assumed to be hot. Then he filled me in on our release altitude which had been less than 400 feet at an airspeed of 60 knots. I called back to Cu Chi and ordered another Flame Bath rigged. Then we tried again. This time I came through at 80 knots on the money, used the second line above center, and released that "hummer" at 400 feet even. Bingo! But that was not the only altitude and airspeed combination used. The faster you went, the wider the spread of the flame area. But there were times when a wide spread was not desirable.

On another drop on a different day, I had to drop some Flame Baths at much lower altitudes due to friendly troops in the area. I do remember bringing one ship back with the paint bubbled on the bottom of the tail boom. I caught hell from the crew chief for that. The heat from the napalm had bubbled the paint because we were dropping from less that 75 feet for fear of hitting friendly troops. On my best shot, I manged to hit a cave entrance on the side of Nui Ba Den about the size of a standard garge door. All three drums went off inside the cave and I got an instant "attaboy" from the troops on the ground that had been under fire from that cave.

Choice of Weapons

As we medically evacuated soldiers, or cleaned up after major confrontations, a number of weapons were left unclaimed. At some point the second platoon started collecting the extra weapons. When I became the Platoon Leader, I was offered a choice of weapons to supplement my 38 caliber pistol. I picked out a M-1 carbine, a M-16 rifle, an M-203 new at that time, with an M-16 rifle barrel over an M-79 grenade launcher barrel, and a .45 caliber sub-machine gun. Then I had the problem of where to put it all. It didn't fit in the cockpit. We didn't have a neat little under-the-seat-storage area like you have in commercial aircraft. Worse yet, they each needed different ammunition, clips and magazines, and you couldn't get the ammunition from Supply. So, unless you were trying to impress some new guy, our 38's and maybe an M-16 slung over the back of the pilot's seat were all we normally took along.

Eventually the Division Commander decided to have

us turn in all extra "hardware." A good move actually. There were guys in the field that needed those weapons a lot more than we did. Each time I got stuck on the ground, my .38 was all I had with me. Fortunately, I never had to use it. I am told that I would have been better off throwing it for the "shock effect" rather than trying to hit someone with a bullet from the dumb thing. While I had those various weapons, I tried them out. From the cockpit none were particularly useful. I couldn't reload a variety of clips and magazines while flying, and the M-230 was an accident waiting to happen. All we needed was to accidentally hit the rotor blades with one of those grenades. If the CO was upset with me for periodically getting little holes in his aircraft from *hostile* fire, can you imagine his reaction if I came back needing an entire new rotor blade because of something I had done myself?

As a platoon leader I had to encourage everyone to turn in their "excess weapons." Not everyone was enthusiastic about that task. Some people stashed a weapon or two and applied for permits to bring them back to the States.

Nighthawk

The "biggie" about being with the Second Platoon was flying the Nighthawk. Now there was an impressive application of the Helicopter. It was awesome. I remember vividly the first time I flew left seat when a gunner fired that beast. I was told it would be loud, but that was an understatement. I was warned not to look to the rear or left because it would ruin my night vision, and I think someone may have mentioned that it would kick the tail of the aircraft around to the right. But nothing could have prepared me for the shock of all that happening at once. You know how you reflexively jump when a loud noise startles you? I think I had said something like "Once you have identified your target you may open fire at will." Well, nothing happened for a few moments. Then, Holy Smokes! It exploded right behind my left ear with a deafening roar like a volcano erupting or some huge prehistoric dragon giving a raspberry right in your ear. Maah! (No wonder the Air Force version was called "The Dragon.") Well, of course the tail was kicked around to the right, *violently*, and with my startled jerking on the controls we almost lost the gunner. From then on I identified targets whenever possible and my fire commands were *very specific*, like, "You have a target? Ready, Open fire, *now*!" I wanted to know exactly when that gun was going to go off. After a few firings you learn to steel your nerves, brace your feet on the pedals, glue your arm to your leg, and press left pedal to compensate for the torque induced by the "Minigun."

Inspections of the airframe on aircraft which carried the "Minigun" bore mute testimony to the torque problem. The metal and bolts holding the tailboom onto the aircraft would crack after a few hours of Nighthawk time. The UH-1 air frame would not stand for more than about fifty hours of Minigun time. But the effect on the ground was memorable. It would tear up every square inch of a football field sized target in three or four seconds. Dust wouldn't settle for several minutes. The North Vietnamese figured it out too. If they saw the telltale searchlight, they would not shoot, not at us nor at the friendly forces on the ground. We had to adopt peculiar stratagems in order to draw fire so we would have a target to shoot at. We would go in high, use only the infra-red search mode, turn on our landing and running lights, then circle like we were a re-supply ship. I remember being so frustrated that I would go down to 200 feet, practically begging the turkeys to shoot at us. Once we drew hostile fire we could mark locations then return fire. After a one or two second burst from the Minigun, everything got quiet.

Occasionally someone who hadn't gotten the word would try to hit us on the right side away from the gun. But that was a mistake! The right side of the Nighthawk normally had an infantry gunner at the door, generally a foot soldier who had served six months on the ground and

Top: Nighthawk
Right: mini-gun
(courtesy John Mistretta)

was good with the M-60. He would locate the ground fire and return fire within a second, keeping fire trained on that target long enough for me to turn the aircraft into the target. Then the Mini-gunner would pick out where the last few tracers were going and hose the area for a second or so. It was very satisfying.

The Nighthawk was a "keeper." Specialist 4, Ace Paradise, a machinist in real life, and a gunner for the Diamondheads built the gun mount and floor plate for the mini-gun. The floor plate took much of the stress off the tailboom. It was a *good* idea, a very effective weapons platform and a devastating weapon. I ended up flying a lot of Nighthawk missions because my night vision was better than most folks', I got good at it, and I liked that job. In about September our unit was flying many more missions than expected, the aircraft and the pilots were getting way too many hours, and we just couldn't keep up with the work load.

Tay Ninh became a hot spot repeatedly during my tour. The Little Bears spent a lot of time flying back and forth to support the 1st Brigade in Tay Ninh, and we ended up with a Nighthawk on call all night at Tay Ninh several days a week. Eventually the CO decided to send a crew up to Tay Ninh to live there. Myself, another pilot and two crewmen were sent to Tay Ninh for an extended period because that would save precious flight hours spent flying back and forth to Cu Chi. We were in direct support of the 1st Brigade 25th Division, so we had some sort of status, rudimentary as it might have been.

We got a nice wooden building with a real roof, and it was next door to the local steam bath. It was also close to the 175 inch artillery battery. I think that was the biggest artillery gun ever included in the Army inventory. It was huge and it was terribly loud. When it went off the concussion shook dust loose from the roof and you could watch small objects in our hootch jump on the shelves. I no longer recall the exact details of the visit, but one night the ladies that work the massage parlor by day, did not get off base soon enough to get safely to their surrounding village homes. So being stuck on base for the night I guess they wanted to get out of the "Office" for a while, and one of the crew men convinced them to spend the night with us. Someone found some cold beer and a party began. There were four of us and about 7 girls, all of whom were ready willing and able to have fun. I ended up with two in the bed in my bunker. Everybody got naked, but at the last minute I remembered they were at least related to the people shooting at us, I had visions of razor blades in private parts, and did not do "the deed." I allowed for a nice massage and some human touch but kept my eyes open until they went back to the massage parlor to spend the rest of the night. The other members of the team seemed pretty cheerful the next day so I guess we all had a good time.

Diverting a Milk Run

One of our ash and trash missions was a sort of routine taxi service to take people to and from the various fire bases in the Delta. It was called a milk run. On one of those we picked up a Lieutenant Colonel who was enroute to an administrative meeting somewhere south of Cu Chi (Tan Anh, I think). We had no sooner gotten airborne when I heard frantic calls for Medevac from a firebase only a few miles away, so I turned the ship towards the firebase and informed the crew we were going to make a Medevac. The Colonel realized we changed course and asked the crewchief what was going on. Once he heard we were going on a mission where we might be shot at he started yelling at me.

From over my right shoulder I heard, "Hey, you turn this bird around right now and take me to Tan Anh!! Do you hear me? DO YOU HEAR ME!"

I said, "Colonel, I just received a request for Medevac.

Some one is hurt and that has priority. Please stay in your seat, I'll get you to Tan Anh shortly."

Over the intercom I told the pilot, "Maintain your heading to that firebase."

I keyed the mike and called Little Bear operations, "Little Bear ops, this Two Six, I am diverting from Tan Anh to pickup a Medevac at XT 547863."

Little Bear operations replied, "Roger that Two Six, call clear, enroute to 25th Evac."

The Colonel in the back was not satisfied, he got up out of his seat to tell me something and the Crewchief warned me, "Die Wie, this colonel is getting out of his seat and he doesn't look happy."

I turned my head slightly, and saw him out of the corner of my right eye. At the same time, we got another call from the ground unit with yelling in the background.

"Little Bear are you inbound? The situation is bad. If you don't get these guys to a hospital soon, they are gonna die, man!"

That was all the incentive I needed.

I told the pilot, "You haul ass to that firebase!"

The Colonel was right behind me crouched over to yell in my ear. He grabbed the rank insignia on his collar and said, "Captain, do you see this? I am a Colonel, dammit! I am ordering you to turn this aircraft back towards Tan Anh right now! Do you hear me!"

At that point, he was yelling loud enough everyone could hear him. His face was flushed and he was hopping mad.

I told him, "I don't give a shit what rank you are. I am in charge of this aircraft and I am answering a higher priority call. You sit your ass back down and shut up, or I'm gonna have the crew put this aircraft down right here. We'll kick your ass out in the jungle and you can hoof it to Tan Anh. We are going to pick up some wounded soldiers. Do you understand me? Now SIT!"

We arrived on the scene at sunset. A Medevac chopper (Red Cross painted on the side and no machineguns for self defense) was orbiting the firebase waiting for things to calm down a bit before trying to land.

The Medevac bird called us, "Little Bear, this is Dustoff, the enemy fire is sporadic, but pretty intense. We have been on station for 20 minutes now, and it's pretty clear Charlie doesn't want us to get in there. Every time I start an approach the enemy fire gets real serious. I advise you not to go in there just yet."

I asked where the enemy fire was coming from and what the situation was. It was desperate, several men had been wounded and they had been bleeding for several hours. It was getting dark fast. I thought it would be better to make use of the visibility to get in and out without hitting any obstacles hidden by the dark of night.

I asked them for a best place to land, told them we were coming in, and informed the Medevac bird. We started our approach. The colonel started getting really antsy, the crew told him to stay seated and keep his seat belt on. As we got closer to the ground, sure enough Charlie started shooting at us. Both the gunner and crew chief opened up with their M-60's. The ground troops increased their suppresive fire, and the enemy backed off. We made a firm landing, not too rough but it did touch down firmly. We were receiving light automatic weapons fire and I felt several hits to the airframe. The infantry unit was bringing four or five guys over on stretchers to put on the aircraft.

That Colonel began yelling at me again.

"Take off! You get the hell out of here! We are under fire!"

And we were, but it wasn't all that bad. While waiting for the last of the troops to be loaded aboard, I looked at the Colonel, he was in a semi fetal position on the seat with his hands covering his head.

We took off and dropped the wounded off at the Hospital helipad. Then I asked the Colonel where it was he wanted to go again and we went on to Tan Anh to drop him off. You might think that was the end of the story, but a few weeks later we got an anonymous medal in the mail. We received Army Commendation medals for a particular incident, so we looked it up to see what it was all about. That Colonel had submitted himself for, and presumably received, a Silver Star, the nations third highest award for bravery in action for that same incident. He submitted us for the ARCOM, Army Commendation medal (commonly called the "Green Weenie"). The ARCOM was given to people for any sort of good behavior, like when a recruit does really well on a physical fitness test. It was sort of an insult.

Landing on a Zippo

A "Zippo" was a Navy patrol boat armed to the teeth and carried two giant flame throwers in the bow. Hence their name, after the popular brand of cigarette lighter, the "Zippo," which had been around since World War II. They could shoot napalm about 200 feet and made a nasty mess on the ground. Their use in Vietnam was primarily river patrol up and down the hundreds of miles of river in the Mekong Delta. They also needed periodic re-supply like everyone else. They were crewed by a few guys, not more than twenty. By pleasure boat standards they were large, but by Navy standards they were pretty small. They did have a landing pad just behind the helm about midway between the bow and the stern.

The first time I landed on one it was day time. We made a pass over the Zippo at about 1800 feet, told them we were coming, and did a high overhead approach. The Aircraft commander was a senior Warrant Officer named Ken Nordane, and he talked me through the whole thing perfectly. Everything went well. We checked for wind direction, told them to "Prepare deck for helicopter arrival," lined up with the boat and the wind, crossed over a second time at 1000 feet even and dropped power to flight idle while starting a wide right hand turn designed to line us up with the boat at fifty feet above the ground exactly 360 degrees later. It worked out perfectly. We came to a high hover about 100 yards from the boat, hovered over and sat down on the landing pad. I noticed they had several long whip-type FM antennae right next to the landing pad, all bent down and neatly tied. We dropped off our supplies and took off into the wind safe and sound.

Several months later, I was the Aircraft Commander. I hadn't landed on a Zippo for quite a while. It was almost dark and the guys on the boat were under fire. So our mission became, "get in and get out quickly." I flew over them at 1800 feet, identified the areas from which they said they were receiving fire and formulated an approach which was generally, but not precisely into the wind, but which would not fly directly over reported "hot spots." A little bit of cross wind is easier to deal with than outright hostilities from guys with guns—right? Then I flew back over them at 1100 feet and started my high overhead approach.

Well, the Vietnamese figured out what I was doing and I think they got ready faster than we did. They started shooting at us just before I dropped the collective and that got on everyone's nerves. They couldn't hit us because we were dropping like a "homesick brick" at about 2500 feet per minute and we were going 90 to 100 knots, but some of them got close enough that we could see the tracers in the early evening light. I remembered the easy landing we had made before, coming over to the boat at a high hover from a hundred yards out. This time there were people taking pot shots at us. I resolved not to do any extensive hover demonstrations. I maintained about 100 knots forward airspeed until the last four seconds, then pulled the nose up to about 60 degrees, and stood the aircraft on its tail for the last 200 yards trying to decelerate from 108 to about 20 knots while avoiding hostile fire. But there was a little extra tail wind and I came up to that boat "hot" landing awfully fast.

The sailors must have thought we would not land while under fire, because they had not taken down their antennae. As we settled on the landing pad the rotor blade chopped them all off! Thankfully when we were on the boat we were out of view from the VC and they weren't going to risk getting too close to the Zippo. A Navy crewman came up and gave us whatever we were supposed to pick up and got their package from us. He was *not* overly friendly. (He was probably the one who would have to put up new antennae.) The good news was, that seeing as how we chopped off their

River boats

antennae, they couldn't communicate any of their hostility to us. So we pulled pitch and got out of there as quickly as possible. I hope the supplies were worth it.

Landing on a Big Boat

Landing on a big boat was a different story. First of all it was far from hostile fire. One day I made a "parts run" to the Corpus Christi Bay, a floating maintenance warehouse with parts and supplies for just about anything. Secondly, it had a regular control tower with a traffic pattern and approach paths. etc. It also sat high above the water and there was always a stiff breeze blowing across her decks. The approach was rather unique for us "bush and jungle" pilots, because we had to land to a point well above the ground and into a strong headwind. It was more than just a little spooky, flying so slow one hundred feet over the water, but as soon as we were over the side of the ship and close to the landing pad it appeared that we were barely moving across her deck, even though our airspeed indicator said we were doing 20+ knots. We set the aircraft down and were immediately re-positioned out of the way in case someone else might come in. Then we went to the on-board PX and were invited to eat in a cafeteria style mess hall. It was nice, but a little depressing seeing what comfortable conditions other people had while we were "out in the bush" without even hot water for a shower. *C'est la vie!* If I had wanted all that jazz I should have gone into the Navy.

Astronauts Had to Hover

July 21, 1969, American astronauts landed on the moon. It was at about 1400 in Vietnam when AFN radio broadcast live coverage of the moon landing. The event caught everybody's attention, even though many of us were flying missions and didn't have time to fully absorb the significance at that moment. Later that evening we clustered around a television in the Officer's Club to watch the replays. That's when it hit us! The astronauts had to hover their lander the last few minutes to find a suitable landing site. Helicopter pilots were experts at hovering. Jet jockeys didn't know the first thing about hovering. So, here was a room full of "hover bugs" feeling their oats about using the same skills as astronauts. There was some partying that night.

A couple of days later I watched an F-4 make bombing runs on a village near Go Dau Ha. When he had finished dropping all his ordnance in an impressive display of firepower and accuracy, a Cobra gunship pilot with a New York accent broadcast this on Guard Radio, "Aaaah, but ya can't *hovva!*" Then he proceeded to hover in front of the target area doing pedal turns to the right and left, Miniguns on full, and firing rockets until there was nothing left but dust and smoke. I think that astronaut stuff inflated our egos beyond all measure.

Red Light, Green Light?

Sometimes we were required to fly exorbitant numbers of flight hours without adequate crew rest between flights. Here in the States, a pilot may only fly about eighty hours in any consecutive thirty day period—and for good reasons. Flight surgeons have examined pilots enough times and under sufficiently different situations to learn about the stress aircraft inflict on the human body: everything from trying to navigate and carry on three conversations at a time, the noise induced stress of aircraft motors or jet engines, rotors, transmissions and aircraft motion, to the stress of landing in a confined area have been monitored. From all this data, flight surgeons have determined that at about ninety hours per thirty day period, the body is so fatigued that pilots begin to make judgment errors which in aircraft are potentially fatal to everyone on board. In Vietnam we had the additional stress of being shot at and the inconvenience of somewhat restless nights interrupted by cannon fire and periodic incoming mortars and rockets.

However, there simply weren't enough pilots or aircraft for all the missions. So we flew as many as two hundred and fifty hours per month. You really can't imagine what that does to your body! We could tell in the showers—when we could take one. Probably the most obvious thing was that the backsides of pilots with over two hundred hours in a thirty day period were bruised black and blue from the waist to midway down the back of their legs. Less obvious was the sort of trance-like state we walked around in for weeks at a time. More serious was the loss of judgment, and the keen edge of our reflexes. Its effect was insidious because you didn't realize it was happening. When a pilot made a fatal judgment error, many times it resulted in a number of deaths, the entire crew paying the price. Most often it was just the discomfort and bruised backside that made us moan at the CO.

It was September or October that I went way over two hundred hours for a 30 day period but kept flying every day. One morning after coming off night flight duty at 2300, (we flew one week of days, and the next week nights), I got up at 0530, took off at 0600 and continued flying until 1800. I was too pooped to party anymore that day, and my poor little butt was sore, but as I called into the Bear Pit for parking instructions, I was informed that someone was in a terrible fire-fight near the Top Hat and I was to offer assistance. So, we refueled hot (with the engine running), re-armed and called for instructions.

The first mission was a medical evacuation of eight American wounded which got us back to Cu Chi after dark. Then they asked for emergency flare support to continue fighting at night. So, off we went again, picking up twenty flares and a full load of ammunition. When we arrived on site, the Air Force OV-10 Bronco spotter was on station and had taken control of the air support. Bronco pilots tended to be "hot dogs," but everyone knew they were good at their jobs and they had earned a lot of respect from all of us. (It was even OK that they couldn't hover.) We dropped flares at his direction for over an hour while the battle raged below. When we were out of flares, we headed back for more, refueled and returned to the battle. This time the jet jockeys were inbound and we were told to "hold" slightly east of the firefight to keep out of their way. The FAC (Forward Air Controller) in the OV-10 was good and seemed alert, so we followed orders. I was instructed to hold in a right hand orbit five miles east at 3500 feet.

The plan was that as soon as the F-4's were on station at 20,000 feet, we would drop a flare to mark the position, then they would make a sighting run and line up for bombing runs from North to South. Keep in mind that these guys come in from 20,000 feet at 450 to 500 knots and expect to pull out of their run at 500 feet. That is a very tricky operation at night. (At 500 knots you are going about 100 feet every second. A miscalculation of just four seconds means you bite the ground.) Also, the flares do burn out, but while they may be invisible, their little parachutes keep them falling slowly cluttering up the sky. If a jet jockey smacks into one of those things at 450 knots, he is going to loose the airplane. So, here in the middle of this three dimensional circus is the FAC roaring around at 250 knots, directing the fighter jets, listening to the ground commander's frenzied calls for assistance, and trying to keep the rest of us out of each other's way. He was one busy dude.

I was worn out. My raggedy little tush was so sore I

couldn't get comfortable, and my eyes refused to stay open. Even toothpicks wouldn't have helped at that point. My eyes closed several times and I kept jogging myself back to reality, but the right hand turns and steady popping of the rotors were putting me to sleep. Just before they closed all the way I saw a red light and a green light separating. Why would a red light and a green light be getting further apart? What was it? My guardian angel gave my brain the shot of adrenaline it needed to start exploring in a dreamy way. *Suddenly I knew.* I opened my eyes, hit the cyclic hard to the right and dived. I looked out the left window just in time to see the OV-10 veering away in a steep left bank. I could see the lights in his cockpit! (Aircraft have running lights: green on the right side, red on the left. So, when an aircraft is coming at you, you can see them both. If it is coming fast, the lights will seem to be getting further apart—*quickly*.) A very close call for a mid-air collision. He had inadvertently climbed up into my assigned orbit. That was *too exciting*. We were awake. That was one of those nights when you change underwear before you go to bed. The next day he came and looked me up to apologize. He had needed a change of drawers too!

Cambodia at Night

One type of mission I flew regularly during my tour in Vietnam was "Flare Ship." Each flare was a cylinder about six feet long filled with a magnesium alloy which burned very brightly. It had a fuse and a long detonator cord made of metal wire. We would pick up a full load, fly to the site where more light was needed, pull the cord and kick the flare out of the aircraft. A small parachute would slow its descent, and as the magnesium caught fire, it would light up an area the size of a football field for three to five minutes depending on the altitude from which it was dropped.

There were a variety of missions which would use that lighting technique. The two principal ones being to light up a target area for Air Force jet jockeys to strafe or bomb at night, and the second to light up an area so our troops on the ground could see outside their perimeter to find the bad guys shooting at them.

Dropping flares for the guys on the ground was pretty straightforward: find the site, contact the Ground Commander, and drop the flares as he requested. Sometimes you could tell immediately that it was a significant combat multiplier for them, and other times we were too late, or they were surrounded by so much jungle, it didn't make any difference. For one two week period during September of '69, we kept dropping flares around the same area with marginal success. So we started following the bad guys with our "Night Hawks" using their huge xenon infra-red searchlight. The North Vietnamese were escaping across the river into Cambodia. They would strike at our ground troops in a semi-circle around a bend in the river as a natural border between the two countries along "the Angel's Wing," 75 miles northwest of Saigon.

I took it upon myself to track the turkeys. It is hard to track anything at night, especially from 400 feet up. We kept losing them in the jungle. So one evening when I was flying Nighthawk, I talked it over with four other crews on night missions in the same area and we decided to take all four ships with as many full loads of flares as we could muster and do our own little raid. First we flew to the river where we had seen the VC disappearing, then west for a couple of minutes and found ourselves over the Angel's Wing where we thought we could see a large clearing in the jungle. It was big enough to see at night. We climbed to about thirty-five hundred feet and dropped everything. We found a huge supply depot just across the border. It had Quonset huts, rows of trucks, jeeps, tents, and lots of boxes of what we assumed to be ammunition.

Then we got caught! We had our transponders on with friendly codes as was standard procedure (7700 I think). The first thing that happened was that when we climbed to 2000 ' we showed up on radar everywhere. Saigon tower called on "Guard Radio" to advise us that we had crossed the ADIZ (Air Defense Identification Zone), and were inside Cambodia. They ordered us to return to Vietnamese airspace immediately. We did not call anyone to identify ourselves as Little Bears, nor did we return the call from Saigon. We weren't done yet. We continued to putter around and check out what we had found. The next call was from Saigon again, but this time it was to advise us of a "bogey" approaching from the west. A Bad Guy aircraft? We knew it had to be Russian because the Vietnamese didn't have aircraft. So what was this idiot going to try and do? Here we were with four aircraft, one of which was a Nighthawk armed to the teeth with a GE Minigun, and three others armed with machine guns. It could have been a HOUND or HIND aircraft!

Was this guy going to try his hand at air to air combat against us? Must be something wrong! We had only heard rumors about the Russian HIND helicopters, including that they carried armor plating. Another was that they had Radio Altimeters which kept the pilots well aware of their exact altitude above ground. Whatever it might have had, we were convinced that the Minigun could take care of a HIND (if that was what it turned out to be). So we all went to blackout—all lights out. (That means you turn off all lights, inside and out: no position lights, no navigation lights, and no rotating beacon.) It is very dark out when you do that, and very difficult to see your wing man, so we separated to different altitudes. I went down low keeping the Minigun al-

ways pointed towards the approaching bogey. The gunner
went to the IR mode and watched the sky like a hawk. One
of the aircraft at middle altitude kept his lights on as a lure
as we headed slowly back towards Vietnamese airspace, everyone just hoping the bogey would try something so I could
let him have it with that Minigun. We all had our fingers on
the circuit breakers to pop the lights back on. (We had to be
able to identify everyone, good, bad or otherwise before I
could shoot.) And our pathfinder minigunner had his fingers
on the trigger.

We had about five tense minutes before Saigon called
again to tell us that we were back in Vietnamese airspace
and the bogey was gone. After the first few "whew's" of
relief we all got angry. "What's the matter with that dip-
stick. Chicken. C'mon, let's go get him." But we had had
about as much fun as we could handle for one night, so
we went our separate ways. Our report of the large cache
of supplies did not alarm nor surprise anyone. I got the
distinct feeling it was old hat to the brass. I think it was
following that mission I started to become disillusioned
with our overall purpose in Vietnam. But there went my
chance to be an Ace. I never got to engage an enemy aircraft in air-to-air combat.

Our little foray had the effect of letting the brass know
some of the pilots were getting brazen. A few nights later I
was flying Nighthawk in the same area and the VC made
another raid on a small outpost south of Tay Ninh. I got there
in time to break up the fight. We came in like a Medevac ship
at about 1800 feet with all our running lights on and started
a slow circling like we were going to approach. We knew
they would shoot at us if they thought we were just a supply
ship. They did. Then I opened up with the Minigun and
caught them with their proverbial pants down. They wouldn't
shoot at us anymore even after we went down to about 300

feet. The gunner found them with the IR searchlight and we followed them all the way to the river. We caught them in the river with the Mini-gun, but when we crossed the river still shooting at an enemy on the run, we were called by call sign, "Little Bear Two-Six. This is Saigon Tower on Guard. You are to break off and return to Tay Ninh now! Saigon out." Not much to argue about on that one. They had my number. We broke off the engagement and headed back to Tay Ninh.

I had barely touched down at the ready pad when someone came out to tell me to report to the Brigade Commander in a briefing tent. Boy was he mad. He "ripped me a new one," threatened Courts Marshal and everything! It seems as though we were not to shoot at the enemy under any circumstance after they crossed the river. That Colonel did not want to hear anything I had to say about them being the same ones who had just shot up one of our (and his) outposts. "You stay clear of the ADIZ!" he commanded. I went back to the aircraft in ill humor, shut it down and sent my crew to bed.

Getting Shot Down

With all that fooling around at low altitude and all those bullets flying my way, it was inevitable that I would sooner or later get shot down. I did—three times! Being "shot down" comes in a variety of flavors, some more serious than others. All of mine were relatively benign. Without going into a lot of detail, let me try to describe what happens in the cockpit when things get "hairy." On one fine morning with just a trace of that ever present tropical haze, we were flying a VIP, a Brigadier General, when out of nowhere we felt several rounds rip through the belly of the aircraft. I was the peter pilot on that mission, flying right seat with an Aircraft Commander who had been "in country" for eleven months and had never taken a hit on any aircraft he flew. He probably had close to 1000 hours of flying time, had been promoted to CW2 (Chief Warrant Officer second grade). He knew he was hot stuff. He refused to address any officer below the rank of Major by anything other than their first name in spite of the regulation which specified he would address all commissioned officers by "Sir" or their rank and last name: e.g. "Lieutenant Finch or Captain Garrity."

Anyway, along came these three or four little bullets and "Mr. Cool" went nuts. He was making emergency calls, ordering everybody to do a hundred things, asking me to find emergency landing areas, and pin-point our location on the map—generally freaking out!

I noticed two things: First, the aircraft was still flying, and second, several of our instruments, including the transmission fluid, were now reading zero. Not a good sign. But what the heck? At least we were still flying. Plus, seeing as how he was the designated Aircraft Commander and flying at the time, he was supposed to be looking for emergency landing areas. When I pointed out to him that we had several gauges out of order, I saw that he had frozen stiff on the controls. We were in a gentle descent heading more or less towards Tay Ninh, but needed to regain some of our lost altitude and turn left to make the traffic pattern at Tay Ninh some ten miles away. I tried to talk to him, but he wasn't listening to anyone. Finally I yelled at him loud enough to be heard without the headsets. (I think that was when the General finally asked if everything was OK?) I told the AC he needed to shake out of it before I "popped his seat." (There is a small lever behind the pilot's seat in a Huey which allow emergency access to the pilots. By popping the lever, the seat would in effect fall backwards, and you sure can't fly in that kind of posture.) He slowly came back to being afraid but at the same time, reasonable. He told me our transmission fluid, which cools and lubricates the transmission, was gone and that the entire transmission would seize in a few moments. That meant that all those gears in the transmission would be so hot from friction that they would fuse together and lock themselves into one position. Then, of course, we would have fallen out of the sky like a "home sick brick."

He started shaking, so I took the controls and headed us for traffic at Tay Ninh. I wanted the thing to land, but inside a perimeter was preferable to somewhere in the jungle. I maintained 1000 feet and 80 knots and called for special "straight in" landing instructions to get us to a landing pad as quickly as possible. We managed a reasonable approach to the third brigade pad where I set it down quickly but smoothly and told our VIP (a General) we were grounding the aircraft until a thorough inspection could be performed. As we shut the aircraft down, the rotor blades had almost stopped turning. The transmission finally froze jerking us around about 90 degrees. That young CW2 had been right. Once again the angels had protected me. A few minutes later my legs and feet started shaking uncontrollably. I guess I finally got scared.

Stealing a Fridge

After I found out we couldn't have fresh meat because we had no refrigerator, I started looking everywhere for one. One day while we were in Tay Ninh, I found six of them in wooden crates in the storage area behind the PX. I asked who they belonged to and was told they belonged to the Special Forces guys on the Cambodian border in an area referred to as the "Elephant's Ear" They didn't even have electricity up there. So what use did they have for six big refrigerators?

The next day I was to fly an aircraft with the tail numbers 346. My gunner was pretty good at rigging loads and didn't think one refrigerator would be any problem. Besides, these things were in wooden shipping containers, ready to go. So we got some white reflective tape and taped the letters 346 so they looked like 848. When we flew by the warehouse area we dropped a rigging net into the yard. We refueled using the call sign "Little Bear 848" letting the pilot make all the calls while the gunner went to "rig one 'frige for sling load." After we had refueled, we flew over to the storage area, hovered in and picked up the fridge and the gunner who was not about to be left behind. Then we hovered over to the road, set down long enough for the gunner to climb in and called for departure. Well, the PX had seen what we did and called the tower to prevent our departure and have us arrested. By the time Air Traffic Control got the word, we were on our way.

"Little Bear 848, this is Tay Ninh Tower on Guard. Return to the First Brigade pad immediately. Your departure clearance is revoked." Well, he was on the International Emergency Frequency now, so I couldn't totally ignore him. I called saying, "Tay Ninh Tower, this is Little Bear 26. Can I be of assistance?" He tried to tell me what was going on and that Little Bear 848 had just committed some sort of theft. I allowed as how that was perfectly awful, and would report 848 to the CO as soon as we got home that night. Half an hour later I hovered over near the mess hall to drop off the fridge, but Little Bear Ops was demanding that I report to the CO, ASAP. So we dropped off our sling load then landed in the Bear Pit. I always conducted the post flight inspections personally with my crew, but this time I left them to do it while I reported to the CO.

At first he was so mad he wouldn't even let me talk. He didn't stop yelling until someone told him we had a refrigerator. He looked at me serious for a moment and asked what had happened. I told him about the mess daddy's complaint, the six or seven refrigerators waiting for the Special Forces who didn't even have electricity, changing the tail numbers on 346, and snatching the "fridge" in broad daylight. He looked me over for a minute, told me to stand in the corner of his office, and picked up the phone. He called the Battalion Commander and the Cu Chi airfield commander and told them he did not have a Little Bear aircraft with the number 848, that it must have been some other outfit trying to implicate us.

He turned to me and really chewed me out: "You will not make any more midnight requisitions while assigned to the Little Bears. Is that clear?" Then he told me to get out. The last thing I saw as I saluted and turned around was a smirk on his face.

Medals We Didn't Get

There was a saying in Vietnam that for every medal you got, you would earn two. It was really a matter of who saw what you did and whether they would be willing to write it up. In Vietnam no one had a lot of extra time for writing up awards on people they hardly knew. Most of my time in the Second Platoon was spent on single ship missions out where no one else wanted to be. I remember trying to medically evacuate some guys from the top of Nui Ba Den at six o'clock in the morning. The mountain was fogged in from half way up to the very top. The helipad was at the top of the mountain which we couldn't see, and it was surrounded by sixty foot trees. I had landed on it a couple of times, but always in clear weather. Two other aircraft had aborted attempts to land and were circling around in the area. They advised us that the fog got thicker as you approached the mountain, and that it was suicide to try to land until the weather cleared. While I understood that, there were some guys who were

wounded and in desperate need of medical attention down
there. I told the crew we were going to attempt a landing
by coming in at a dangerously slow airspeed aimed at the
place where I thought the helipad was located. They were
to keep all eyeballs peeled and report as soon as they saw
a hint of trees or anything solid.

That part of Nui Ba Den is very steep and covered by
huge boulders. If we hit one of those we would be dead.
We backed off about half a mile and started an approach.
Through the chin bubble I could see we were not properly
lined up with the land marks I remembered, so I swung
around to the right to try again. The men on the ground
reported that they could hear our rotor blade noise and we
seemed to be to the south by a couple of hundred yards.
That reinforced my own idea of the landmarks below us.
We began a second approach. I slowed our airspeed to
about 30 knots—not a real good idea because we became
sitting ducks for anyone with a pistol, rifle or pea shooter.
The fog shrouding the mountain from our view was also
hiding us from people on the ground. But there is a limit
to any hunter's patience. At some point the VC either saw
us through the fog, or thought they could locate us by
sound accurately enough to start taking pot shots. We were
under fire once again. We entered the fog at that point and
I had to concentrate on what I was doing. I brought the
airspeed back to about 20 knots. My eyeballs were agog
watching to see if a tree might materialize a few feet in
front of us, hoping I would have enough time and room to
turn right or left to avoid hitting it. The guys on the ground
called to tell us they could hear our rotor blades *and* rifle
fire. The pilot acknowledged their transmission, and had
the foresight to ask if we sounded like we were properly
lined up for an approach. The answer was a yes, and that
we sounded very close. While that was good news, I was
too busy to do anything but fly.

We kept hovering into the fog hoping we would see something soon. Then the gunner spotted trees just below us. A quick glance through the chin bubble reinforced that. We were about ten feet over the tree tops, but no helipad was in sight. Then the guys on the ground called to report that we were off to the south of the pad but very close. I canted right just a little and asked them to check again. That time they were able to see the trees being blown around by the rotor wash. They told us to hover more to the right. Finally the helipad lights materialized through the fog just a few feet off our right side. The crew chief was elated. "Come on over to the right, *Di We!* I see the pad!"

Boy was I glad to set that chopper down. My gloves were wet with sweat from tension. We picked up three soldiers, turned around on the pad and made a maximum performance climb out through the fog. A few moments later we were in clear weather headed for the hospital at Cu Chi. I think that was the "hairiest" flying I did in all my tour. No one was there to see that effort, so it went unrewarded except for the fact that three guys were given a better chance for survival.

Little Bear 26 on Nui Ba Den

Another day of unrewarded antics also involved Nui Ba Den. It was some time in August. We were asked to re-supply some guys half way up the side of the mountain. At their particular location the mountain was very rocky and steep. It was a hot day with a high density altitude, and the ship we had was barely able to hover at that altitude. We had to ferry the supplies in two loads. The first time we went in was okay. We shot the approach to a point in space near the location of the troops, hovered slowly over to them and dropped supplies out the left side of the aircraft.

The second trip was a bit different. The bad guys had watched carefully, and when we shot the second approach they were waiting for us. At about the time we slowed to 20 knots they opened up on us. Let me say that it is inter-esting to try to hover on the side of a mountain under any circumstance. When you are being shot at in addition to the difficult flying conditions, you have this urge to say, "Naah, let's do this some other time." It would have been so easy to drop the nose and dive over the side of the mountain to safety. From that height we could have been up to 100 knots in a couple of seconds. We did not run. We hovered over to the drop point taking a couple of hits along the way, and the crew unloaded the rest of the supplies. We did it quickly, but we didn't run for safety. Then the gunner finally said, "That's it. Get us out of here!" I didn't need to be told twice. We dropped the nose over the side of the mountain. No one was there to witness that activity except the soldiers on the ground. But they were the reason all the rest of us were there. I never forgot that they did not have the option of running away over the side of the hill.

There was Hope

When the movie "For the Boys," starring Bette Midler, came out, I was struck by the very realistic portrayal of the

Vietnam I recollect. I remember well the arrival of "The Bob Hope Show" to Cu Chi during December of 1969. It was publicized for weeks in advance. The excitement was amazing. It was very much like your first memories of Christmas with all sorts of unknowable surprises, anticipation of numerous goodies under the tree, and a sense of family unity. There was a frenzy of activity to build a stage, put in sound systems, and put together dressing rooms for members of the troupe. Every one was looking forward to seeing the show.

A couple of days before they were due to arrive we learned that our company had perimeter security during the visit and would be unable to attend the show. The day before the show at Cu Chi, my platoon came to me with an unusual request. "Captain Finch, we know you are aware of how much we wanted to see this show. Now we find out we have security duty for that day, but we want the Hope show to know we appreciate them. Will you do a leaflet drop on the Bob Hope Show?" Well, would you have said "No?" I didn't. One look at all those sleepy eyed soldiers and my mind was made up.

The next day at about 1600 as I was getting ready to fly security patrols, the guys from all three platoons came over to the Bear Pit with cardboard boxes full of these pathetic leaflets saying "The 25th Aviation Battalion Welcomes Bob Hope to Cu Chi, RVN." "Merry Christmas from the Little Bears: A Co., 25th Avn Bn" and the like. They must have been up all night making those little leaflets, so I was resolved to drop them properly on "The Hope Show." The first and only obstacle was that it would be highly illegal, and I would have to find a way to trick the Control Tower. They had put up a "no fly zone" around the area where the show was set up. I knew that if I were to over fly that restricted zone I would be in hot water—again. I could even have been prosecuted.

As soon as I was given departure instructions, I radioed that I was making a left hand break and was changing frequencies to Saigon. When the Tower called to tell me I was not to make a left hand turn, I had already done so, and swooped over the show area dropping leaflets by the thousand. Cu Chi Tower did call on Guard Radio to inform me of the flight violation, but by then the deed was done.

When we got back some time after midnight, the CO was waiting up for me. I showed him a couple of the leaflets, told him what I had done and for whom, and he never said another word about it to me.

A few months later when that episode of the Bob Hope Show aired on television, Mr. Hope's comment on seeing all the leaflets was "What's this? Snow in Vietnam?" I am sure each of the soldiers who stayed up all night making those things was sure it was worth the effort.

A few years later, in 1975, while attending Saint Martins College, someone had the idea of inviting Mr. Hope to an extravaganza we were planning. So I called him and made the invitation, citing to his aides the time I dropped snow on his Christmas show in Vietnam. He came to Saint Martins and I talked to him about the incident. While walking down a corridor to the stage at St. Martin's, he asked me why we had dropped the leaflets and I explained that the troops had been up all night making them and that I just couldn't let them down. We did it as another way of saying we appreciated what he was doing for service men and women in Vietnam. Yes! It was *well* worth it.

A Memorable Medevac

A particularly memorable Medevac was in a place we called the Bo Loi Woods, a Michelin rubber tree plantation. We had diverted from a resupply mission to do the Medevac and were light on fuel, so we could pick up some extra weight. When we finally got on the ground there were a whole bunch of wounded. I told the crew to just keep piling them in. Those guys had been pinned down since early morning and were tired in addition to the beating they had been taking. We had six on board when the Crew Chief gave me an "up." Some twenty yards away, one more GI was still limping towards the ship as we began receiving fire. I could hear the telltale "crack crack" of AK-47 fire. The Crew Chief started yelling at me, "Get us out of here. We are taking fire." We were sitting ducks on the ground, and had a full load as it was. He was right of course, it was a full load!

Pretty soon, Infantry wounded soldiers were sitting on top of each other, but it was only a ten minute ride to the hospital. I told the crew chief to get that last guy in and I would pull pitch. The next thirty seconds seemed like forever. We could hear the sporadic pops of rifle fire, friendly and hostile. It was time to get out and we all knew it. That last GI got to the skid and looked up at us. The Crew Chief hollered, "We have a full load, *Dai We*. Let's get the Hell outta here!" I turned to see just how full and said, "Get that guy in here!" His leg was so messed up they had to drag him in and it took a few seconds of effort, but he made it. After we got out of the landing zone, I turned the aircraft over to the pilot then turned to see how the guys were doing. They were tired, smelly, and muddy, and in pain, but there were smiles back there. Kind of makes it seem worthwhile. No awards for that, no extra pay, just the thought that you did OK.

Three years later I was the executive officer of a battalion at Fort Polk when that guy walked in to inspect our battalion. He looked at me for a minute and said, "I know you!" After a few minutes of playing "where were you when," he asked what unit I was with in Vietnam. I told him I had been a Little Bear. He got a strange look on his face and said, "You were the pilot who allowed me to get on, when that ship was already full! I was shot in the leg at the Bo Loi Woods in 1969. I was really hurting and it looked like you were going to take off without me. At the last minute a crewman helped me on. You turned around to look at us as soon as we got airborne. Your face was the last thing I remembered before waking up in the hospital. God bless you!" We did OK on the inspection, but I'd like to think it was because we were ready.

Giving the Orientation Ride

The last time I was shot down was a bit more exciting. By December '69 I had turned into a pretty good Platoon Leader, had received every award an aviator had any reason to expect, had been credited with successful Medevacs of over 800 people, and had the respect of a lot of the guys because I had been through every type of situation our company could experience. So I guess it was natural they would want "to put me out to pasture" for my last few weeks in country.

On a day three weeks before I was to leave Vietnam, I was assigned the mission of giving an orientation ride to one of our new "Wobbly Ones." (A reference to the grade, Warrant Officer 1, and the fact that he was a recent Flight School graduate, still wet behind the ears, and a tad wobbly on his flight wings.) We had a brand new aircraft with less than 25 hours on it. It even smelled new.

We started off flying around Cu Chi and shooting traffic patterns at Long Binh, Saigon, etc. while I showed him procedures, hot spots and navigation techniques. Then at about 10:00 hours, I monitored a call for help from some troops near Nuy Ba Den. I offered to assist, and got permission from Little Bear Ops to help with resupply. By 1200 we were decisively engaged and I had flown about four times into one particular hot spot on the north side of the mountain. We had brought in amunition twice and equipment once. We kept receiving hostile fire from one pile of rocks on a ridge line. Even the OV-10 pilots couldn't get in close enough to do any damage, so I called for Tay Ninh to rig a Flame Bath.

I picked it up with the intention of dropping it on the VC on that ridge. The OV-10 pilots who were trying to mark the target kept getting shot up, so I had to rely on my instinct and knowledge of the area to locate and line up on the target area. There was intense fire coming from those rocks. As I lined us up for our bombing run, I could tell we were going to get hit, so I told the guys on the ground and the crew to keep some suppressing fire trained on the rocks.

It was difficult to tell exactly how high the target area was, and I was not sure which hatch mark to use in sighting. But in we went at 80 knots. As I punched off the load I saw why the bad guys were so well protected. It was a cave! The flame bath went right into its mouth. When we came out of the right turn at the top of our climb out, all you could see was smoke. All the flames were inside the cave. The next mission was to bring water to the Pathfinders who had been engaged in this firefight all day in the tropical sun.

This "Wobbly One" and I had been flying sorties into "hot LZ's" (landing zones) all day and had received several hits. So far, they all were superficial skin punctures which didn't bother us much. Then at about 15:00 hours we were trying to make a simple water drop. This was now my seventh or eight approach to that area. On the way in I started getting all this free advice:

From guys on the ground, "Little Bear, this is...Be advised the LZ is hot...blah, blah.."

From other pilots, "Little Bear" you had best...."

And from someone in a C&C bird (Command & Control aircraft), "Little Bear, this is...We've been on station thirty minutes now and advise...."

Then the new pilot started a commentary for me: "You know this is more fun than watching the evening news with Walter Cronkite..."

I smacked him with the back of my hand and yelled, "Shut up!" Then I went to Guard Radio and keyed the mike, "This is Little Bear 26. I know the LZ is hot, we have been in and out of there 10 times today. Now get off the air. We're busy."

"Pathfinder, get your smoke ready!"

Next, I went to the FM radio and tried to contact the Pathfinders whom I was trying to resupply, only to be interrupted again. It was getting hectic. Because of all the hostile fire and some friendly fire ricocheting off the rocks, I had to make a highly unusual approach at high speed, (below the tree tops in several places) with a number of sharp turns, and finally a maximum performance pop-up climb to altitude near the location where our guys were pinned own. Just the flying end of that mission was tough enough. I sure didn't need a bunch of bimbos clogging the airwaves with useless chatter. I told the guys on the FM that I was aware the LZ was hot because I had made several trips into that LZ earlier that day. "Now get off the radio so I can do my job."

I told the Pathfinders to "pop smoke" where they wanted the water and that we were one minute out. Then we started receiving all this hostile fire. The pilot's controls on the right side of the aircraft were shot out and his cyclic was flopping around like a spaghetti noodle. That brought on a fresh onslaught of commentary from the Wobbly One. Now I had all three radios going plus this lunatic in the right seat talking my ear off on the intercom with trivia! Then I saw the yellow smoke just ahead and up the side of the mountain, maybe 400 feet above us. I started my climb while decelerating so as to be at a hover right at the smoke. We dropped the three bladders full of water just as we were at hover, and had just started a pedal turn to head back down the mountainside when an RPG (Rocket Propelled Grenade) came out of the jungle to our right rear and hit the right rear skid. There was a big explosion. It blew off half the skid and punctured our fuel cell. The crew chief started yelling that he had ben hit, lots of instruments were reading zero—including the gas gauge. The ground troops called on the FM radio to complain that we were spilling fuel on them. (Oh Gee. Thanks guys. I would really rather keep it on board for the engine, you know, but somehow that isn't a choice anymore.)

I was the Aircraft Commander and at the only set of controls, so I had to find a place quickly to set us down. I had been in and out of that area enough times to know where there was a clearing in the jungle not far from the protection of some tracked vehicles near the base of the mountain. We went in hot. It probably took one minute and thirty seconds from when we were hit until we were safely on the ground.

A quick inspection showed a number of small arms hits. With a prayer we could get the aircraft back to Tay Ninh, only fifteen minutes away. That was infinitely preferable to staying out in the bushes. So we fueled-up using a 55 gallon drum (enough for about a 20-minute flight) and hobbled over to Tay Ninh. At Tay Ninh we refueled again and hobbled part-way back to Cu Chi, refueled again, and limped home.

When we got the aircraft back to Cu Chi a thorough inspection showed we had taken twenty-eight hits, one of which was a round through the tail-rotor drive shaft. Some of the other hits were the one that took out the pilot's controls, and a round that went through the cockpit just above my left ear at a moment when I must have been leaning forward. *The guardian angels had been watching over me again.*

Had we not turned and dropped the nose of the aircraft exactly when we did, that RPG would have hit the aft bulkhead and I would not be writing this. The Wobbly One got an orientation ride he would not forget. But it's never a perfect day. The CO was upset about my ruining a brand new aircraft and grounded me. My orders for rotation out of Vietnam had arrived, and he didn't want to have to explain my loss at that late a date. Three days later I was told to fly up to Tay Ninh again for some sort of ceremony. The Division Commander was there and presented me and the new Warrant Officer with Silver Stars. I was speechless! Later I heard that I had actually been put in for a Medal of Honor, but it had been down graded to the Silver Star. Even that was more than I had ever dreamed possible. What an honor. Apparently one of the guys on the C&C bird that I had told to shut up, was the Brigade Commander of the troops I was trying to help. He was very appreciative and informed the division commander of our actions. I guess I finally made it as a Little Bear. I hope Major Robert "Spook" Grundman and the other guys who didn't make it where proud of me.

A few days later I boarded my "Freedom Bird" out of Vietnam!

POSTSCRIPT

My tour in Vietnam lasted from January 29, 1969, to January 29, 1970—exactly 365 days.

I logged 1,269 hours of combat flight time in my one year in Vietnam, and that was average for a Little Bear: 409 hours of night gunship time, 204 hours of VIP lift ship, 250 hours of combat assaults, and 406 hours of "ash and trash" (including one hour of Celestial Navigation). I also Medevac'd over 800 wounded personnel. In all those hours of flying, there were thousands of good take-offs and landings and at least two bad ones.

I lost four aircraft while I was flying: Little Bear 256 (transmission seizure following hostile fire), Little Bear 186 (crash landing off north end of runway 33 at Cu Chi), Little Bear 769 (crashed into rice paddy on a maintenance flight), and Little Bear 346 (26 structural hits and one RPG in right rear skid).

My "total KIA," the credited number of enemy killed in action, is 875.

Under my command, three crew members were injured (only one seriously): a crew chief was shot in the butt with shrapnel when the RPG hit #346; a gunner was on drugs and when told to "drop flares," he pulled the cord carelessly allowing the cord to whip around in the wind, hitting him in the eye; and Bill Bailey, the maintenance officer, broke his arm when thrown out of #769 on impact.

I received several personal awards, including the Silver Star, the Distinguished Flying Cross, 29 awards of the Air medal, the Bronze Star with V device for valor, the Vietnamese Cross of Gallantry with Silver Star, and five Army Commendation Medals.

The "Little Bears" received four unit awards. In 1968, they received the Meritorious Unit Citation, the Valorous Unit Citation, and the Presidential Unit Citation. In 1969, we received the Vietnamese Cross of Gallantry with palm.

For those who might have read this and asked how I made it through, I too have often asked that of God and of myself. Why was I spared? Not only was I spared during the various encounters retold here, but also from those I omitted, including several which claimed lives.

I did not become a whacko, malcontent, or shoot people in the streets because "of what the war had done to me." I led a normal, happy, and highly productive life, was placed in positions of increasing responsibility, and was soon promoted to the rank of Lieutenant Colonel.

In 1986, I was assigned to Washington D. C. as Inspector General U. S. Army Military District of Washington. In 1988, I was assigned to the Armed Forces Inaugural Committee as an operations officer for the inauguration of Mr. Bush. That was a demanding job where I worked as many as 18 hours per day and after the election, 22 hours per day at least once a week. In early 1989, I was assigned as the Operations officer of the 101st Signal Brigade where I worked on disaster relief for hurricane Hugo and helped plan the invasion of Panama.

On Saturday October 28, 1989, I slipped and fell in my house, hitting my head three times before coming to rest on the floor. I could not get up and was in tremendous pain. That same young man so willing to face adversity to help others in 1969, was now helpless. I had suffered a near fatal stroke. I was paralyzed on the left side, unable to speak, and had lost all my short-term memory. At Walter Reed, U. S. Army hospital, an MRI scan showed the doctors an area of brain damage the size of my fist. Three weeks later, psychometric testing showed I had lost all my temporary memory and all ability to do math. You have heard the saying, "Of all the things I ever lost, the one I miss the most is my mind." That was me in 1989.

Not one to stay still too long and not being one to give up easily, I was soon able to get around a little and talk again. The doctors were amazed at my recovery. The doctors came by my room in teams of 6-10 to check out the walking miracle. They told me they did not understand how I was able to walk or talk or remember anything. They kept asking my name, address, and phone number. One of them looked at the MRI scan and said within earshot, "I don't give him 18 months to live." Do you have any idea how devastating that is? I was already struggling just to get back to normal and that guy gave me the idea it wouldn't make any difference.

The doctors started putting all these limitations on me, "You will never be able to..." All kinds of things. (I could never be an effective member of a team again, I could never supervise people or activities again...) They were the experts and they were telling me how limited my future was and all the things I would never be able to do. They were never able to pinpoint why I had the stroke or how I was able to improve so rapidly, but they all had opinions on how limited my recovery would be.

One of my friends, Mark Durant, visited me in the hospital. He asked me if the doctors could explain why I was able to speak, walk a little, and remember things. I said, "No, they can't." He said "I can, Joe. It's because the Lord isn't finished with you yet and if I were you I would get right with the Lord soon!" I was invited to know the Lord, Jesus Christ personally, and I accepted. I did not know that my younger brother, Geoffrey had been praying for me to do that for 22 years! Then someone read to me Isaiah 40:31. (Those who trust in the lord shall renew their strength) and I read about Lazarus. And, I believed.

I finally got my spine up and told the doctors it wasn't up to them to decide what I would, or would not be able to do. I wasn't too sure myself of what I would be able to do, but at least now I had hope, and the promise that God would help me. What I did know was that my life had changed dramatically. The Army did not want me anymore. I was told I would be discharged under a 100% medical disability program, and I knew it would be very hard to get a job—ever again.

I went through four months of physical therapy and began attending church regularly.

During 1990 I joined the church choir and was healed in ways I can only attribute to a loving Heavenly Father. The church needed people to help with construction of a choir room in what was a raw, unfinished basement. I offered to help and got to know other committed Christians who were helping build the church. My hand and arm coordination were polished through the various tasks I was given. Martin and Cleonia Olson were exemplary Christian leaders and great guides for my incipient faith. Their constant prayerful approach and appreciation for all the good that God had done set a tone for my faith and became my example for how Christians act in daily life.

Later, the church needed someone to organize all the music. Not too hard is it? Except that all the choir music starts with the same thing: Jesus my Lord, Jesus my Savior, Jesus my Rock, so I had to put a word then letters in sequence. One of the things that didn't work was my ability to sequence alphabetic characters, and I really struggled with which letter followed another. I remember singing to myself over and over that grade school alphabet song "A B C D, E F G..." Eventually it got easier to remember which letter came before another. I never thought about it at the time but God used that circumstance and that little song to get my memory back in working order.

I had never sung before and still don't sing all that well. I found that God doesn't need you to be a gifted musician, or even very talented, just willing. I was willing.

One more obstacle to my recovery was that I was not very steady on my feet and was deathly afraid of falling. At night, I was terrified to walk around the house for fear I might fall and have all that pain again. Our choir music was all in the basement of the church. It is not just dark down there, when the lights are off it is dark as the pit of hell! Without the lights on, there is no path for light to reach around the corridors down the stairs and into the passageways to give any light at all to the basement. One evening as I was going to organize the music, the door to the corridor into the choir music room accidently closed behind me leaving me terrified and in utter darkness. There was no light. Fighting rising panic, I started singing softy" I will call upon the Lord, who is worthy to be praised, so shall I be saved from my enemies, I will call upon the Lord." You know what, I didn't fall. I made it across that room (25 or 30 feet) in total darkness, found the light switch on the far wall and turned it on. I have not been afraid of the darkness since.

Another feature of my memory that did not work well was my math skills. I couldn't do simple additions and subtractions or multiplications at all. One time, I had to make change for someone on a minor transaction in the church dinner line. I couldn't do it. Finally, with tears in my eyes, I explained to the lady I wasn't able to do math anymore. She said, "It's okay. We'll do it together. She took my hands and gently, patiently showed me how to count out the change again and again until I had it right.

I couldn't get a job largely, I think, because the word was out that I had been medically discharged and would only live a few more months. No one wanted to hire me, train me, then have me die, and be forced to start over again. I attended bible study classes and lots of church events. I could feel myself getting stronger, and could almost measure the improvement in my abilities daily. Without money coming in, my disability pay was not enough to sustain us in Northern Virginia. Each month we withdrew more and more money from our savings, until in October 1990, it was all gone. My wife, Monika, had been working two or three jobs at a time in order to bring in some money to pay our mounting bills. Every Sunday I took whatever money I could get together, 5 or 10 dollars so I would have some money for the offering plate. Life was difficult for us at that time. I was praying regularly for help, and in retrospect, the Lord was helping me more than I could have asked. I had received no favorable responses to over 200 resumes, and it was not clear to anyone that our situation was improving. In October, Monika, through tears of anguish, told me that I would have to get a job doing something ASAP. I told her that just as she had faith that the Veterans Administration would send me a check, in spite of how inept we had found them to be, I had at least that much faith that the Lord would provide me with a good job and that we were going to have to be patient and wait on the Lord's timing. November was an awful month, we weren't eating right anymore. On the first Friday of December, I was hosting the bible study group at our house. I found a box of stale crackers and sent my daughter Tanya to the store to buy us a dip. When Monika came home she saw the plate of crackers and a dip, and asked what was going on. I explained and she stormed out of the house saying she would not be humiliated by having people over and not being able to feed them something nice. The next day was Saturday and I explained to my family that we had to all pray together for help because I had been praying by myself and that had obviously not been enough. So we all prayed together for help in getting me a job. The next day, Sunday, I went to church and found Bruce Gearhart staring at the ceiling.

I said, "Hi Bruce, I see you are contemplating higher things." He responded that his work was classified and he wasn't able to talk about it. I said I understood because I too held a security clearance. He said, "Oh Really? Would you like a job?" I said yes, and Bruce introduced me to Ken Cummins that same afternoon. Ken and Bruce took my resume and re-wrote it to fit a job they had recently opened. They told me that they would hire me after an interview with the owner of the company and after they agreed to a salary. As I got ready to go home, I asked what I should tell my family. Ken said, "You may tell them you have a job starting in just a couple of weeks." Elated hardly describes the sensation. When I got home I explained to Monika what had happened and then told the kids. Tanya asked, "Daddy, does God always answer prayers that fast?" I said, "No, but when He does you praise Him for it!" The job paid handsomely and we went from poverty to surplus in just a couple of months. Monika stopped working three jobs and backed down to one. Things just seemed to kick into high gear.

At the end of 18 months, the Veterans Administration called and asked me to come in for a re-evaluation physical so they could determine if I should still be paid 100% disability. I reported to a young doctor at Walter Reed. He looked me over, asked a couple of questions, and said, " OK colonel, I'm going to put you back on active duty!" I protested that they had unceremoniously thrown me out as being incapable of performing, and gave me a bad enough prognosis that I couldn't get a job, and now that I finally had a good paying job, I was just supposed to jump to! and do what they said? "I hardly think so. " He said, "I'm sorry colonel but I have no choice. There is nothing wrong with you. The Army invested a lot of money in your training and schooling and there is nothing to prevent you from performing full duties." I asked to see a senior medical officer, explained to him that the hospital would look stupid throwing me out as a hopeless case and then trying to fully reinstate me 18 months later. He did a little more thorough examination and found there are some lingering discrepancies, but agreed that I could be allowed to choose whether to re-enter active duty or be retired. So I was medically retired in 1991 with 30% disability.

Amazing recovery? Nope, I say it is a Miracle. I firmly believe the Lord helped me recover. As we often hear said, "The Lord works in mysterious ways. " I have seen some of those mysterious ways and I can only conclude that there is a loving, giving God who really does care for us and who is alive today.

Today I am fully recovered and back at work. Doctors are still not able to explain how I got all my memory and other faculties back, and one doctor went so far as to say, "After looking at your MRI, I have no way of explaining how you got from where that shows that you were, to what I see today. " I do. The Lord wasn't finished with me yet. Perhaps He spared me so I could write this account of one average guy's experience. Perhaps there is some other purpose of which I am not yet aware. Perhaps it is to encourage other veterans, or so that some of those young men whose lives I touched in Vietnam might call me and find out that they are not forgotten. Perhaps it is a way of closing one chapter of the book of my life on a pleasant note. God only knows.

I would like to encourage other veterans to write down their memories as a means of closing the chapter and reconciling that experience with the rest of what is good in life.

For those who read this and think it was easy, remember that, this book, *Angels' Wing* only discusses a few days of relatively mild activities. The other 330 plus days were full of sights and sounds you wouldn't want in your worst nightmares.

There were terribly sad moments in my tour. I lost friends and associates and saw young men die as we were medically evacuating them on our ship. I saw a man tortured to death, saw a man pushed out of an aircraft 1000 feet above the ground, and a whole lot of things I do not dwell on. Those are things I will leave for another story, but this book would not be complete without mention of the following people:

Two members of my platoon died in a crash; WO-1 Michael Drake and WO-1 Leonard Sugimoto. I heard the radio call announcing to the world that "Little Bear 214 has just crash landed at our site!" I knew more or less where they were flying, looked Northeast from Tay Ninh, and we saw the fire ball where their aircraft was burning some 10 miles away. We cranked up and flew over as fast as we could. We nearly got into retreating blade tip stall at 124 knots close to the ground. Ours was the first aircraft on the scene to try to offer help but there was nothing we could do for them at that point. The two pilots were burned almost beyond recognition. The tragic loss of these two young friends touched me in a way I am not able to explain. There just aren't any words that fit. It is the hard part about war and something you just never get used to. Andy Anderson, who flew on the recovery mission the next day, made this entry in his journal: "Those blobs of burned flesh that had been men. I had to help put them in body bags. I'll never forget that smell. We put them on board and started their last long ride home. God bless them. I just wish it seemed worth it. Two more lives wasted."

From the official army death data entry:

LASTNAME: DRAKE FIRSTNAME: MICHAEL JOSEPH
IDNO: 370502822 SVC: A COMP: V RANK: WO GRADE:
W1 MOS: 100B AGE: 21 HOME: ROYAL OAK ST: MI
CASDATE: 19691216 CAS1: C1 CAS2: B CAS3: 5
BODY:—CTRY: VS PROV: 22 LSVC: 00 BIRDATE: 19480515
RACE: C REL: RC MAR: M SEX: M CIT: 1 TOURD:
690308 PANL: 15W LINE: 062 REFNO: 4558 PDATE: 6912

LASTNAME: SUGIMOTO FIRSTNAME: LEONARD JAMES
IDNO: 570700752 SVC: A COMP: V RANK: WO
GRADE: W1 MOS: 100B AGE: 22 HOME: GARDENA ST:
CA CASDATE: 19691216 CAS1: C1 CAS2: B CAS3: 4
BODY:—CTRY: VS PROV: 22 LSVC: 00 BIRDATE: 19470126
RACE: M REL: BO MAR: M SEX: M CIT: 1 TOURD:
690510 PANL: 15W LINE: 065 REFNO: 4555 PDATE: 6912

Two weeks prior to that incident, Drake and Sugimoto had asked me not to assign them night missions, as they both believed their next night mission would be their last flight. I juggled the schedule as best I could for awhile, but everyone was flying way over the limit in hours. I finally ran out of options. I had to assign them a night mission, and they crashed into a tree on approach at night. They flew that mission in spite of their private terror. They are heroes.

Another friend who didn't make it home was Sgt. William Kenneth Hunter, the black door gunner with the big smile who saved us all several times by quickly returning accurate gunfire when someone on the ground tried to shoot us down:

LASTNAME: HUNTER FIRSTNAME: WILLIAM IDNO: 249687725 SVC: A COMP: R RANK: SFC PP: + GRADE: E6 MOS: 12B40 AGE: 28 HOME: ORANGEBURG ST: SC CASDATE: 19700506 CAS1: A1 CAS2: G CAS3: 7 BODY: — CTRY: VS PROV: 02 LSVC: ** BIRDATE: 19461029 RACE: N REL: BO MAR: M SEX: M CIT: 1 TOURD: 690921 PANL: 11W LINE: 113 REFNO: 27065 PDATE: 7005

Last, and most painfully, my close friend, Donny Kilpatrick. Donny was not a Little Bear, but a friend from OCS and flight training who had just been married to his high school sweetheart, Bonnie, while we were in flight school.

LASTNAME: KILPATRICK FIRSTNAME: DONALD ROBERT IDNO: 180367651 SVC: A COMP: V RANK: CPT PP: + GRADE: O2 MOS: 1981 AGE: 22 HOME: BETHLEHEM ST: PA CASDATE: 19690902 CAS1: A1 CAS2: B CAS3: 4 BODY: —CTRY: VS PROV: 22 LSVC: 02 BIRDATE: 19461213 RACE: C REL: RC MAR: M SEX: M CIT: 1 TOURD: 690128 PANL: 18W LINE: 024 REFNO: 24416 PDATE: 6909

Donny was not scheduled to fly on 2 September 1969, but the guy who had been scheduled to fly that aircraft, Roy P—, got the "willies" and could not fly. He had sort of a premonition of disaster that completely unnerved him, made him a nervous wreck, and he was not fit for cockpit duty. Donny stepped up to take Roy's place. On approach to a landing zone, a .51 caliber machine gun fired a single round before the gun jammed. That one bullet hit Donny in the face. He never knew what hit him and surely felt no pain.

No! Vietnam was not a lighthearted, fun, experience and most of what happened to me has, thankfully, been erased by the passage of time. But most of us felt an over-whelming sense of loyalty and duty and we endured those hardships hoping and expecting that it was for the good of our country. We believed we were doing the right thing. The ancient Greeks called it *agape* (Ah-Gaa-Peh) a love of something greater than ourselves. We were willing to put ourselves in harm's way in order to serve a greater cause. In many cases young men gave their lives to save or help others.

I thank God I am alive and well and that I was able to grow past all the nightmares. I am reminded that even in the midst of the terror that was war, the Lord used me for something good. Each of those successful MedEvac's made a real difference. If you don't think so, ask the guys who were evacuated!

"Greater love hath no man than this, that he lay down his life for his friends." John 15:13

As a last note, there are a number of dedications, me-morials and tributes to the soldiers who fought in Viet-nam. The helicopter has gone on to fire fighting missions, traffic and weather roles, and a ubiquitous world wide role in aero medical evacuation. Many of those roles were de-veloped and refined by the young pilots in Vietnam who were willing to try anything to better help the infantry soldiers on the ground. It seems fitting that a memorial be dedicated to the helicopters themselves. And, the Fulton County Flying Club in Canton, Illinois has done just that. They found that the old helicopters we flew in Vietnam were pretty well worn out, but Alan Dilts and Jim Hartford wanted to create a memorial to the helicopters that flew in Vietnam. They did some research and found that a non-profit organization could buy an old Army UH-1 helicopter for a dollar. So they bought one, had it shipped to the Fulton County airport, read through all it's old logbooks, (Good old Army, kept the paperwork). They researched its role in the war, found it had been a Little Bear aircraft from its arrival until it was nearly destroyed. They restored it to look like it had when it was in service as Little Bear 819. That gracious old bird—just like Little Bear 186, which we crashed—performed hundreds of Medevacs and spared lives on her last flight, and now looks as good as new. It now stands as testimony to the enduring legacy of the helicopter's role in Vietnam.

I am so proud to have been part of that.

Ron Leonard, Diamondhead 085, has created an exceptional web page (*www.25thaviation.org*) with photos of Little Bears, Diamondheads, and our living area in Cu Chi. Ron has opened communication and created a healing touchstone for those who want to find meaning from the experience of war.

One thing the intervening years have done is open my eyes. Each new hand I shake is a blessing, a story, and a history waiting to be told.

Is there nothing worth fighting for?
Yes. Agape, Filios, and Eros. Agape most of all.

SOMETHING ABOUT HELICOPTERS

T his is not intended as a helicopter operations manual, but certain terms need explanation to follow the story.

Primary flight controls: Primary flight controls are duplicated on the left and right sides of the cockpit so that a helicopter can be flown from either seat. The primary flight controls are first: The CYCLIC: an aluminum shaft that sticks up out of the floor between the pilot's legs. It controls the nose pitch, up and down, by movement fore and aft, and roll of the aircraft to turn right or left. The cyclic moves in a full circle of fore and aft, right and left combinations. To go into a climb you pull back on the cyclic and push forward to dive. To turn or "bank" to the left, you push the cyclic to the left. Similarly, to turn right, you push the cyclic right. Normally...usually...almost all the time, control movements are gentle and you do not need to push the control stick very far.

"Proper pilot technique" refers to the ability to smoothly operate the controls with gentle but firm movements, especially on the cyclic. The grip of the cyclic has a variety of triggers, push buttons, and toggle switches to control

various operations required of that particular aircraft. If you have cargo slung beneath the aircraft, the cargo hook release also is on the cyclic grip.

The second primary flight control is the COLLECTIVE which is another aluminum shaft on the pilot's left side. It moves up and down to increase or decrease the amount of power applied to the transmission. Pulling up on the collective changes the pitch of the rotor blades and increases power to give you lift. Helicopter pilots say they are "pulling pitch" when they pull up on the collective to get airborne. The collective also has the throttle which is rolled to the left to increase engine RPM or to the right for off. Normally an automatic fuel flow governor controls the engine speed much like the cruise control on a car. After the engine is started and brought up to cruising RPM, the pilots do not have to fiddle with it except under extreme conditions.

The third flight control is the PEDALS. There are pedals for the left and right foot to counteract the torque of the engine and transmission. They control yaw, or the left and right movement of the aircraft's nose. If you loose the pedal controls, all control becomes very difficult. The nose drifts or pitches right or left every time power levels change. The principal use for pedals in a helicopter is during a hover. Pedals keep the nose pointed in the direction you want. Both hovering operations and departures require well coordinated movements of all the controls.

Who is doing the flying: The person operating the controls or actually flying the aircraft, can vary during flight depending on the situation. The Aircraft Commander normally sits on the left side of the cockpit. He designates who will "fly" the aircraft. To turn the controls over to the pilot he states, "You have the 'controls,'" or to take control back from the pilot states, "I have the 'controls.'" In my experience, time spent at the controls was split 50-50 between the pilot and Aircraft Commander. The only exception to that was when an AC did not trust a pilot's skill. When that occurred, a flight standardization pilot was assigned to provide additional training and enhance the weak pilot's skills.

Hovering: Flight instructors are quick to remind students that a monkey can be taught to hover. While that might be true, the task becomes quite difficult when it is necessary to carry on two or three conversations at the same time. That is what we all had to do. We had to tell the control tower our intentions, explain to the ground operations folks what we were doing and plan the flight, all the while hovering around to position the aircraft for the next event, e.g. parking, departure, picking up supplies or wounded soldiers. In the event of a wind from the left or right side, hovering becomes tricky in that you must keep pressure on the pedals to counteract the wind. Think about that for a moment and you will realize one of the problems of hovering. The wind is never constant. It normally gusts at varying speeds causing you to change the amount of pressure on the pedals. It could get real busy at a hover even when you were not being shot at. A helicopter, like most modern aircraft, has several radios and an intercom for talking to the crew.

Pre-flight and Post-flight inspections: Before the first flight of the day each aircraft is inspected for air-worthiness in what is called a pre-flight inspection. The Army version of the "pre-flight" is a very thorough inspection of all major components: tolerances on couplings of as little as one ten-thousandth of an inch, amount of play in rotor blade assemblies, fuel lines, electronic components, a check of all rivets in the fuselage, each structural bolt and a myriad of other details. Air Force pre-flight inspections were not as thorough, and they were performed by the crew chief, not the pilots. You might ask how we could check bolts? Each one was painted with a small dab of paint from the center of the bolt to the surface where it was attached. If the paint was cracked, it meant that the bolt had turned somehow and the maintenance crews would have to re-set and certify it. One of those many nuts and bolts was the retainer nut, on the top of the rotor mast, referred to as the Jezus Nut. If that came off in flight, you were going to meet Jesus. A thorough pre-flight could take 45 minutes. One of the principle reasons for the differences between the Air Force and Army inspections is, if all else fails in most Air Force aircraft, the pilot can eject and parachute to safety. Army helicopter pilots do not have that option. Therefore the pre-flight was thorough. As an aircraft was shut down at the end of the day, we performed a post-flight inspection which was also very thorough. In Vietnam this was an even more critical inspection because we never knew when we would have to scramble out to the flight line and get the aircraft started in a hurry. So, after each post flight, the aircraft was set up for a quick departure under emergency conditions. The main rotor blade was tied to the tail boom, and cowlings were placed over a couple of critical items. But in an emergency, we could start the aircraft in a few moments.

The Chin Bubble: Most helicopters have a clear plastic window below the pilot and aircraft commander's feet which dramatically increase visibility, and are invaluable in hover operations.

Velocity Not to Exceed: Helicopters, like all aircraft, have a *VNE.* That is the maximum airspeed you can safely fly before something bad happens. In our training helicopters, the front windshield would collapse at about 100 knots. Therefore VNE was set at 90 knots to give student pilots a margin of error. On the "H" model Huey, VNE was set at 120 knots. At 126 knots we got "retreating blade tip stall" which meant a total loss of lift on one side and the aircraft would roll violently to the right. Pilots learn these things and try not to practice them...ever.

Seat Belt System: One last peculiarity worthy of mention is the seat belt system. In a commercial airplane you wear a lap belt much like the one in a car. In helicopters and fighters, you wear shoulder harnesses in addition to the lap restraint. It is all designed to keep you in the seat in the event of a crash. They are all buckled together on a large piece of leather at your stomach which constrains your movements in the cockpit and makes it very difficult to get out in a hurry.

Autorotations: Helicopters have one unique advantage over fixed wing aircraft, they can autorotate to a soft landing if the engine fails. Where fixed wing aircraft typically, must keep substantial forward airspeed to keep from falling out of the sky, helicopters can use the momentum of the rotor blades to slow their descent and airspeed to perform a pin point landing. If the engine quits, the transmission disengages and the rotor blades are able to free wheel. The momentum of the blades and the airflow throught the disk of the rotors will keep the blades turning at more than adequate speed for a normal autorotation landing.

Communication: Radio transmissions are made by selecting the "active" radio with one hand, and pressing a trigger switch on the cyclic grip all the way in. To talk on the intercom only, you press the same trigger switch half way in. Radio procedures as taught in Flight School were not what we used in Vietnam, and flight rules, even in good weather, were far different in a combat zone. These vignettes highlight some of the ways we adapted Flight School training to the conditions we found in Vietnam.

The last thing I will say about flying is that you need to understand that a helicopter pilot fresh out of Flight School doesn't know much about how to fly. He knows even less about how to *fight* a helicopter in war. At best, he knows how to do a pre-flight check, and start and shut down a helicopter in *daylight*.

Helicopters fly low and slow. Many of their missions, like hovering to pick-up wounded soldiers, make the helicopter an ideal target; it is easy to hit and inflict multiple casualties and is usually followed by the arrival of more "targets." That's a fact VC counted on. So helicopters were very vulnerable, and because they saved Americans and hurt Viet Cong, they were a high priority target.

Our survival rate in the face of all these odds is a testimony to the competence of our instructor pilots, team work of the air crews, and American ingenuity. We learned some lessons the hard way, but we adapted quickly and did a lot of things right.